Dynamic coherence of Continental Philosophy

Bart Nooteboom

Dynamic coherence of Continental Philosophy

Aspekt Publishers

Dynamic coherence of Continental Philosophy
© Bart Nooteboom
© 2023 Aspekt Publishers
Amersfoortsestraat 27, 3769 AD Soesterberg, the Netherlands
info@uitgeverijaspekt.nl-http://www.uitgeverijaspekt.nl

Cover: Lisa Dijkhuizen
Interlining: BeCo DTP-Productions, Epe

ISBN: 9789464870619
NUR: 730

All rights reserved. No part of these pages, either text or image may be used for any purpose other than personal use. Therefore, reproduction, modification, storage in a retrieval system or retransmission, in any form or by any means, electronic, mechanical or otherwise, for reasons other than personal use, is strictly prohibited without prior written permission.

Contents

Introduction 07

Flow of knowledge 24

Language. 47

Ethics 59

Existentialism and poststructuralism 76

Society 91

Conclusions 104

References 109

Introduction

Continental philosophy (CP) has no clear definition. It descends from the philosophies of Kant, Hegel, other German idealists, and Schelling, Kierkegaard, Adorno, Heidegger, Nietzsche, Derrida, Wittgenstein, Gadamer, Foucault, Lyotard, Rorty, Piaget, Levinas, Buber, and others. To give some historical perspective, in figure 1 I give a timeline of some relevant philosophers.

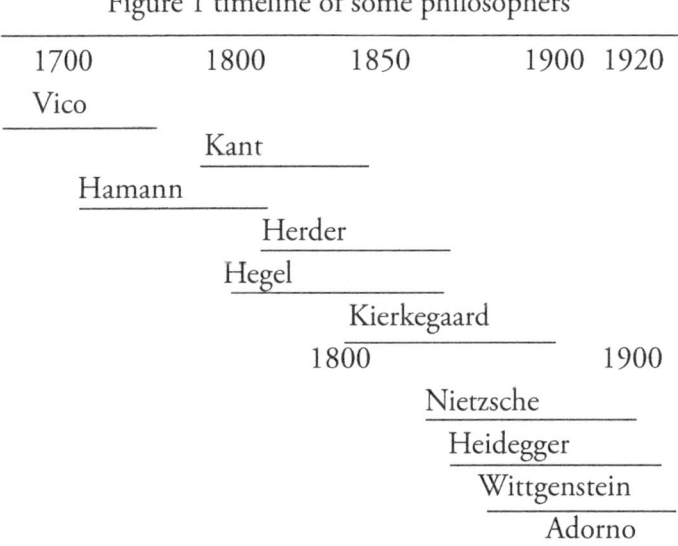

Figure 1 timeline of some philosophers

One can appreciate some elements of a philosopher's work and reject other elements.

Continental Philosophy (CP) is fragmented, with comparable but often conflicting bits and pieces. In this book I propose that what they have in common is that they seem to be on the way to dynamics, but do not quite reach it, and often leave it implicit, or try to deal with dynamics in static terms. Rather than lamenting that a photo is not a film, let us talk film. Development occurs in knowledge, ideas, language and meaning, existence, ethics and society.

Isn't my talk of dynamics, change, just another form of metaphysics, replacing the realist metaphysics of objects with a discrete, fixed identity, by their flux? Perhaps, but some metaphysics, defined as not amenable to empirical validation, is inevitable. How do you validate love, meaning, loyalty, trust, justice, and so on?

I do not wish to suggest that there is no dynamics in previous CP. Hegel told of a process of development of a 'world spirit', culminating in some horizon of fulfilment, and used the notion of 'phronesis' to characterise the process of developing a life.[1] Marx, of course, outlined the economic dynamics of society. Merleau-Ponty spoke of the 'flux' of life, in the interaction between body and mind.[2] Kierkegaard, and later Heidegger, saw the individual not as given, but as developing in the world. The Hermeneutics of Gadamer speaks of scientists following a 'tradition'.[3] Derrida told that 'deconstruction' moves on to transformation in some new context. Nietzsche told of the 'genealogy' of morals, and Foucault of the genealogy

---

1 Tamineaux 1994: 45
2 Merleau-Ponty, 1964: 57
3 Madison, 1994: 305

of suppressive institutions. Postmodernism saw knowledge not as a fact but as an 'event'.

However, I claim that this book carries dynamics further, clarifying some of the puzzles in CP, such as its opposition to 'presence', fundamentalism, given identity, separation of subject and object, mere instrumentalism of relations, hypothetico-deductive and encompassing scientific systems, suppressive institutions, 'logocentricity', disappearance of the individual in social and political systems, fixed meanings and interpretations.

CP is supposed to be pragmatic, useful for guiding policy and conduct, but that is difficult to do if you deny any form of truth, as some recent continental philosophers do. Several CP philosophers employ the Aristotelian notion of 'phronesis', practical philosophy where general concepts are adapted and modified according to the context of action. Here, I think of Levy-Stauss's notion of 'bricolage', muddling through. Practical conduct requires debate between different perspectives, and that requires some notion of adequacy if not truth. I maintain Dewey's notion of truth or adequacy as 'warranted assertability', which is pragmatic, including the practical use of a concept and its origin and development. I claim that the dynamic perspective resolves conundrums in previous philosophy, and helps to understand knowledge, language, identity, ethics and society, as I try to show in this book.

CP is contrasted with Analytic Philosophy (AP). It is said that AP is oriented to 'explanation', in science, and CP to 'understanding', in wisdom. More than natural science, social science and philosophy indeed need discourse. Science desiccates human experience, CP gallops off with it. Science is dominated by technique. Marcel gave the following striking characterisation: 'Technique shows the calculative mind in action. .... The idolatry of technique is really a metaphysical hostility to our vulnerability before the incalculable chance of being.'[4] From my own experience (in econometrics) I know that technique may be necessary, but it is not sufficient, and to enable it, may distort the matter at hand for the sake of enabling measurement. Formalisation can improve the analytical power of a theory, and the art is to balance that with the distortion it may bring.

Taken literally, the distinction between explanation and understanding puzzles me. Good explanation requires understanding, and understanding helps to explain. Take present physics. Mathematical formulae explain the mysteries of quantum physics, but physicists admit that they don't understand it, they are mystified, and don't like it. Explanation shows the perceived causality of things, and understanding connects that with other knowledge, intuitions, history, and contexts. Plausibility requires coherence with other knowledge, history and practice. In this book, I discuss and use Aristotle's multiple causality of action, which, I claim, yields both explanation and understanding of human conduct.

Explanation in science used to be claimed to connect with reality as its foundation, and that is a delusion, as Kant already taught. Understanding is coherence within a wider system of cognition that is based on itself, does

---

4 Desmond, 1994: 137

not have any outside foundation, but is self-referential, based on some 'background knowledge' that has come to be tacit and taken for granted, evolving from experience in the world.

Some label CP as what analytic philosophers detest, who celebrate logic, clarity of concepts, and scientific methodology, which they see lacking in CP. However, some ideas form a bridge between Analytic and Continental philosophy. One is Frege's distinction between 'reference' and 'sense'. I will return to that in the chapter on language. And while Habermas, for example, is a continental philosopher, he gravitated to some extent to AP in his later work, pleading for rational discourse.

I appreciate the work of Kierkegaard and Nietzsche, who are widely considered as 'irrationalist'. In characterising my work, however, I avoid the term 'postmodernism' because of an unpleasant experience with some colleagues at a university, who held that 'any opinion is as good as any other', rejected any notion of 'truth', and refused to enter into debate. I agree with Rorty that there is not a single theory, but a 'multiplicity of language games', but I claim that there can still be theory that connects the games. Renouncing theory, as Rorty does, one loses all grip on society[5]. He pleads for 'inspirational liberalism', and militates against cruelty and suppression, but did not specify how. As Bernstein (2003:136) said: 'if there is no theoretical analysis, he falls into 'mindless activism'. As Taylor (2003: 176) put it, 'Rorty's escape from 'mediationalism' (representationalism) is lost in a

---

5 Best and Kellner, 2003: 303

kind of night where all views about Mind and World are shrouded in equal darkness'. This is reminiscent of Hegel's dictum that in the night all cows are black. One can still have theory while admitting its contingency on preestablished background assumptions, with debate among people who share the same perspective, and achieve some intersubjectivity. It is sometimes even possible to 'cross' what I call 'cognitive distance'.

At first, I thought that CP was anti-Enlightenment, in opposition to the dominance of rationality, and it was that, as early as in the 17th-18th centuries, in the anti-Enlightenment philosophies of Vico, Herder and Hamann[6]. But Kant, Hegel and Marx were Enlightenment philosophers, in the sense that they strove for rationality, Kant in the present, in knowledge and ethics, Hegel at the end of the full development of the 'World Spirit', and Marx in the production and equitable distribution of the material means of existence, to be brought about by Communism. [7]

An important stream in CP is that of 'Critical Theory', from the 'Frankfurter Schule' of Horkheimer, Adorno, Habermas and others[8]. They criticised the Enlightenment with its 'totalising', universalist, foundationalist ambitions, but they admitted that social freedom is inseparable from Enlightenment thought. They engaged in 'Internal Criticism', not of the aim of rationality but in the way

---

6 Berlin, 1976
7 Sherrat, 2006
8 Sherman, 2003

the Enlightenment failed to achieve it.[9] After the war, the pressing question was how Nazism could have developed in a society that was supposed to be rational.

For me this is misleading. I would not plead for a society that is purely rational. Emotions also have a role to play, as I will discuss later. Nazism had a highly emotional appeal, of nationalism, racism and violence. I do not mean to shed rationality, but life needs a combination of reason and emotions, which can derail, while I deplore that now reason is increasingly neglected.

The old view was that if life and society are not dominated by reason, there seems to be no sense to life. Can we then avoid nihilism? Acceptance of emotions and reflexes is not nihilism, but is positive, part of life. With life, one is offered an opportunity, and one should make choices and take responsibility for them, as Kierkegaard argued. It is not despair at the loss of fixity, certainty of religion and metaphysics, but delight in it, in facing the challenge. This is not raising oneself to the level of God. Where does life come from? One can think it comes from God, if one insists. But it won't help in life. If God gave us life, it was to challenge us, and we can't expect any help.

Freedom is needed to exercise the challenge of life, even in a state that endeavours to exclude individuality, since it engages in the universal, what people have in common, instead of their unicity. Kierkegaard accused Hegel of effacing individuality in the grasp of his system. This objection is reminiscent also of Schelling.[10] This

---
9   idem
10 Wirth, 2005: 17.

theme of difference played a central role especially in the later French CP of, among others, Lyotard, Derrida, Foucault, Deleuze, Levinas and Buber. Levinas and Buber will be discussed in the chapter on ethics.

This dedication to accept difference between people is one example of the coherence in CP. It is also similar to the plea of Taoism, of limited rules (wu-wei), to leave room for uncertainty, and be resilient to the vicissitudes of nature.[11] This is easy to say. Societies can't do without rules, and our present society is far more complex, requiring more rules, than the simple agrarian society of Lao-Tse and Zhuangzi. In our society, liberals seek to minimise rules, but in capitalist society, a paucity of rules increases economic inequality. The challenge is to find a minimum of rules that still blocks poverty and exclusion.

A late member of the Frankfurter Schule is Habermas[12], who still strove for rationality, in a debate between people, in what he called 'communicative action'. In his commitment to reason, Habermas neglected emotions and their role in living life, in conjunction with reason, and their adaptive role in evolution. Only a small part of the brain is dedicated to reason, the rest to emotions, routines, and reflexes that are largely subconscious. They are not irrational but non-rational, and developed in the struggle for survival, in evolution.

Figure 1 shows that the anti-Enlightenment philosophers Hamann and Herder were virtually contemporaneous with the Enlightenment philosopher Kant, and were

---

11 Zhuangzi, 2007
12 1982, 1984

preceded long before by Vico. Vico was an early opponent of Descartes, and proposed the two fundamentally different sciences of nature and behaviour.

A relatively recent stream in CP is what Sim (2000) called 'The new scepticism', which militates against old philosophies that claimed universality and the achievement of truth on the basis of universal foundations. This scepticism claims that every thought or theory is perspectival, depending on basic background assumptions that may vary, and that one cannot step out of to achieve objectivity. The background assumptions are the outcome of an historical process in which culture is built up and shared within groups, and different between groups. This is found, in different forms, in Nietzsche, Gadamer, Foucault, Derrida, and Rorty. In fact, one finds it earlier, with Hume, who claimed that in science we cannot achieve certain truth, though in ordinary life we disregard that[13]. Causality does not entail that cause and effect are necessarily connected, identity is nothing but a bundle of perceptions, in a perpetual flux and movement, and one cannot be certain of the stability of nature. Rorty claimed that also scientific theories are mere 'language games' played in communities that share their perspective, and are no more true or better founded than literature. Hume already rejected identity as fixed, and saw it as perpetual flux and change. I am tempted to say: with Hume, who needs Derrida? But Derrida deepens Hume' scepticism.

CP is supposed to be pragmatic, practice-oriented and thereby akin to the American pragmatism of Dewey and

---

13 Williams, 2003: 70

James. As a result, several continental philosophers have also been called pragmatists, such as Nietzsche, Heidegger and Wittgenstein[14] This pragmatism may yield a bridge between AP and CP, since AP is utilitarian, aimed at solving problems, although it tends to lock itself up in unexamined assumptions and dogma. CP is rooted in practical issues and experiences. Habermas claimed that theoretical knowledge is rooted in practical interests[15].

Not all features discussed in this book are adhered to by all Continental Philosophers.

Continental philosophy strives to be interdisciplinary, connecting philosophy, history, sociology, and social psychology. It is historically aware, and intent on the 'genealogy', development, of things, with the work of Nietzsche [16] on the development of morality as an example.

In fact, interdisciplinarity is scarce. There is an evolutionary argument against it. In evolution species cannot mix. If they did, and there were no limit to it, and all species would mix, there would in the long run be only one species left. Similarly, as discussed in the chapter on knowledge, in science disciplines are specialised in 'research programmes', defended by 'hard cores' (Lakatos), and this achieves the focus of disciplinarity. On the other hand, it is often by combining different disciplinary views that novelty arises.

---

14 Malachowski, 2013
15 Critchley, 2001: 117.
16 1966

Figure 2

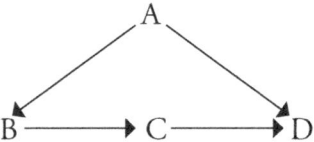

From early on, with Adorno, CP rejected causality, as belonging to the old foundational philosophy, neglecting human factors, and being the handmaiden of cursed science. One intuition is that of causality as mechanical push, later it became a notion of effect, influence. A purely formal notion was the 'INUS' condition, with factors that were individually necessary and collectively sufficient. Multiple factors were allowed, including inhibiting factors, and the lifting of them. There can be strings of causes, including intermediate ones.

This is illustrated in figure 2. Here, A affects B which affects C, which results in D. A does not affect C. An example is a sluice. There is a difference in the level of water on the two sides, and sluice doors keep it from flowing, until they are opened. This is shown in figure 2.

Causality may also be reciprocal, as in people interacting, the human being exploiting nature and getting climate change in return. Action evokes reaction. In the case of a violinist, the musician's talent and training affect the quality of playing the violin. In the case of an athlete, the shoes enhance or obstruct the talent and training of the athlete.

I adopt Aristotle's highly pragmatic multiple causality of action. The 'efficient cause' is the agent, the 'final cause' its purpose, the 'formal cause' how, by what knowledge and skill, it pursues it, the 'material cause' by what means, the 'conditional cause' under what conditions, such as markets and institutions, and the 'exemplary cause' as the model followed.

One can extend this causality by those causes that cause, in turn, the conditional cause, for example, such as institutions, climate, and nature, or the psychological and societal causes of goals. This is illustrated in figure 3

Figure 3

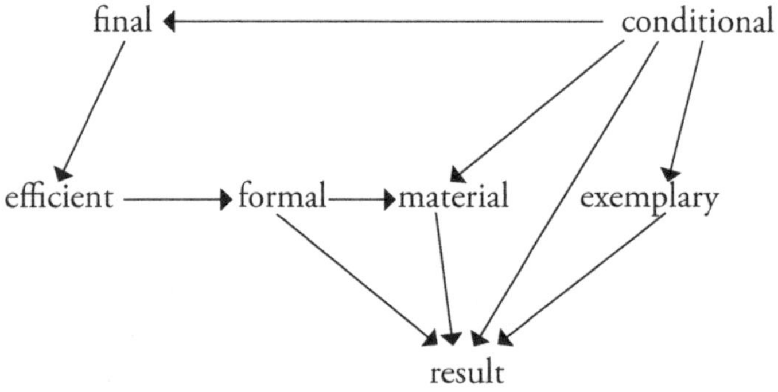

```
final ◄─────────────────── conditional
  │  ╲                    ╱ │ ╲
  │   ╲                  ╱  │  ╲
  ▼    ╲                ▼   │   ▼
efficient ──► formal──►material  exemplary
                        │
                        ▼
                      result
```

It is customary to see multiple causality as adding up causes: A + B + C: The star violinist had a good violin, great talent, and was well trained. The Olympic runner had great training and good running shoes. Often, causes are multiplicative: AxBxC, or a mixture of additive and multiplicative: A+BxC. One cause can influence, reinforce or limit the other. In the multiplicative form, if one cause is zero, the whole is zero. In fact, perhaps in most cases one cause is conditional upon one or more other causes. The conditional cause can facilitate or inhibit the final cause. For example, the market may not yield a demand for a product. It can also affect the material cause, by forbidding the use of certain materials.

This causality does not imply a return to the old foundational, representationalist pretention to mirror nature, but coheres in the language game of explaining action. Aristotelian causality forces one to consider individual conditions of purpose, means, ways, conditions and skills, which depend on time and place, and is thus inherently historical, fitting in Continental Philosophy. I was struck by the view of Vico that we need to find the 'causas' by which things are as they are, and come about, and not stop at only seeing its static properties.[17]

Adorno pleaded for 'interpretative philosophy', avoiding analysis on the basis of lawlike causality. Concerning causality, however, I claim that Aristotle's multiple causality is apt for understanding the human being in society. I think this contributes to the humanisation of the analysis of humanity and society.

A central feature of Continental philosophy is that history matters, and that universals are misleading.

Another central feature of Continental philosophy is the recognition that the individual, the subject, no longer is a pre-formed outsider looking at the world, but develops in the world. This is expressed in Sartre's slogan 'existence comes before essence'. This idea was proposed earlier by Heidegger. Another example is Simone de Beauvoir's

---

17 Berlin, 1976

view of feminism: the view that men entertain is seen not to derive from some male essence that makes them superior, but derives from the experience of subservience imposed by patriarchal society.

I propose that 'Existence comes before essence' leads to a dynamic view of the individual, as not having a fixed identity, but developing it, with the prospect of death. This presented a problem to the criticism of Adorno: if the self is part of the totality of society, formed in interaction with it, how can it escape from the conceptual constraints and ideologies that society imposes, and at the same time be critical of it?

Most CP rejects the old separation and opposition of subject and object. However, they cannot merge, as Adorno thought. There remains what I call 'cognitive' distance, and what I would now include as 'emotional distance', between people. This distance, when crossed, yields learning, not only in the sense of acquiring existing knowledge, but also discovering new knowledge, transcending the old.[18]

An important puzzle in CP is that of existentialism, pleading for freedom and duty of the self to follow one's convictions, taking responsibility for one's life, and structuralism, which focuses on the constraints organisations and society impose. They are indeed difficult to reconcile, yielding a dilemma of authenticity and conformity. We have an urge towards authenticity, but are constrained by society.

---

18 Nooteboom, 2000

To what extent are we bound to ordinary and customary language and thought? Adorno struggled with the notion of transcendence, which sounds metaphysical, which he rejected, while he saw the need and possibility to escape from the static notions of established thought[19]. I call that 'horizontal' transcendence, in expanding the scope of a language game, as opposed to the 'vertical' transcendence of appealing to a higher power of unlimited thought. Horizontal transcendence does not yield absolute, Platonic knowledge, but it is transformative, in what Thomas Kuhn called a 'Paradigm Switch', yielding a new perspective, in what I call 'imperfection on the move': one will never achieve Platonic perfection, but one can achieve new views, even if those are still not perfect.

Another central feature of continental philosophy, is that it is humanistic.[20] There was some humanism in classical thought, and it arose in the Italian Renaissance, partly in revival of classical thought, and came to full fruition in the Enlightenment, in the ideal of autonomy of the individual. It entails that the individual can rationally manage by itself, without imposition of authority. Horkheimer and Adorno argued that this is an illusion, and I claim that the Enlightenment's glorification of reason has stunted the human potential for emotions and morality that transcend science and reason.

Sherrat (2006) connected humanism with Hermeneutics, going back to Gadamer, which refers to Hermes, the

---

19 O'Connor, 2013
20 Sherrat, 2006

ancient, wing-footed Greek god of trade and travel. Hermeneutics means 'interpretation' which arises in communication, and has deep roots in ancient Greek, Latin and Judaic thought. For example: do you read the Bible literally or allegorically? The reformation yielded a different reading of the bible from Catholicism. Hermeneutics says that any interpretation of a text or theory is perspectival, resting upon a system of partly tacit background assumptions that developed as part of a culture that people share to a greater or lesser extent, what Rorty called a 'language game'. While analytic philosophy focusses on the truth content of an expression, Hermeneutics looks more at how it is received and arises in life. I will return to it in the chapter on language.

Critchley (2001) connected the distinction between analytic and continental philosophy with C.P. Snow's distinction between 'the two cultures' of science, concerning how things are, and literature, how to live one's life. Science is in danger of becoming inhumane, neglecting the old question what is the good life, and CP is in danger of falling into incoherence and obscurity. Critchley showed that the split is not between English and CP philosophy, but also a split within the UK, for example between Bentham and Coleridge, and between universities.

A philosophical system should, I think, include a theory of knowledge, truth, ethics and morality, language, culture and society, and these form the chapters of the book. I follow this tradition not only because it is customary, but also because in the philosophical system presented here, those parts support each other. I am not against system, as long as it does not pretend to be complete, with objective foundations, and is open to development. They subjects of this book cohere in a processual view of knowledge, ethics, language and society. That is the significance of this book to the field. There is much literature on the separate subjects, but no such synthesis that I know of.

This is a short book, aimed at students, practitioners and professional philosophers. The intended attraction to students and practitioners is that it is brief, avoids jargon, and gives examples from life. The attraction to professional philosophers is that it unifies ideas from Continental Philosophy that before were fragmented. Perhaps the process view expounded is new to some scholars. 'I think the later French continental philosophers were gesturing towards a dynamic perspective, but did not develop it.'

The flow of knowledge

It is astonishing that some philosophers adhere to the old opposition between idealism, which holds that we perceive the world according to frames of thought, and we do not perceive reality as it is in itself, and realism that claims that we do. Those views are both partly right. At any moment we see the world through frames of thought (idealism), but in the interaction of subject and object, our ideas adapt (realism). Here, I use the dialectic, derived from Jean Piaget[21], of 'assimilation' of experience in forms of thought, and 'accommodation' of those forms if that fails to achieve a fit. This is another way of framing the 'hermeneutic circle' of a dynamic interaction of text (view, understanding), by which we see the world, which forms the context of meaning, and context. A new text may alter our perception an interpretation, which in turn alters the context.

Adorno struggled with the notion of metaphysics, which he rejected, and he thought that transcends our current view of things, which he strove for, and called 'transcendence', and the 'negative dialectic' of Hegel. I call it 'horizontal transcendence'. Things have a potential to change, but such realisation and development of potential is not transcendence in the usual sense. Horizontal transcendence is transformation into a new identity, with a new potential, such as a caterpillar that turns

---

21 Boden, 1979, Flavell, 1976 Piaget, 1975

into a butterfly. In ideas, an example is Kuhn's 'paradigm switch'.

What is consciousness? According to Heidegger, Merleau-Ponty and Gadamer, consciousness is, in the words of Merleau-Ponty, a 'mode of being in the world'[22]. But how does it happen in the brain?. Brain scientists do not yet know what consciousness is and where it is. Some say that this is a fake problem as long as we know how it works, in circuits of neurons, with neurotransmitters that inhibit or stimulate connections between neurons. One can observe that with PET (Positron Emission Tomography), which measures brain activity by the intensity of oxygen transported by streams of blood, and MRI (Magnetic Resonance Imaging), that lights up on a screen where brain activity is highest. Thus, in sleep, with a low level of consciousness, the lighting up of circuits of neurons is less dispersed than in waking condition. Coma yields a yet lower form of consciousness, but that is not entirely absent. In drunkenness and druggedness by LSD, the influence of perception by the senses is increased, and in depression or schizophrenia, such influence of sensory perception is lowered. In the first one is overwhelmed by impressions, and one loses the self, with the second one loses oneself in the self. Many of the processes in the brain are subconscious, and partly not felt. One can be conscious of the circuit belonging to some action. One can be conscious of being conscious, but it is not clear how this happens.

---

22   Madison, 1994: 311

Neuronal networks get activated and shifted upon one's moving in the world. The mind is formed by a durable network of neurons that expands and gets refined as one grows old and accumulates more experience. That forms someone's identity, not fixed but in ongoing development, sometimes for the worse.

Greenfield (2000) compared waves of consciousness with throwing a stone in a pond, with extending but weakening ripples in the water. Consciousness can be seen in a momentary lightening of paths of neurons, on the basis of PET or MRI.

Neural networks in the brain may sound like a revival of representationalism, where objects or events are mirrored in the mind as discrete entities. But something must be going on in the system of body and mind. Merleau-Ponty emphasised the unity or 'Chiasm' (crossing), as he called it, of body, ('the visible') and mind.('the invisible')[23] This does not imply that the mind 'mirrors nature'. In the mind, local networks are embedded in the whole of the mind, the 'lighting up' of local networks is partial and parts of the network do not 'stand-alone', but are conditioned by the whole of the mind, in interaction with the body, and have an effect on that whole. A single experience may reverberate through the mind (and the body) and have a durable effect

From the work of Jean Piaget, I developed a 'Cycle of Discovery' ('COD'),[24] which has the merit of showing how the 'hermeneutic circle' might work, in going from experiences accumulated in the past to a new

---

23 Merleau-Ponty, 1964
24 Nooteboom, 2000

understanding. The process has several stages. First, in 'generalisation', an existing practice is carried into a new context. If there it does not fit, variations of the practice are made, tapping from experience. If fit still fails, perceived elements from the new context that are successful where one's own fail, are tried out in the present structure, in 'reciprocation' (so called because vice versa some of one's own practice may also be adopted locally). That will often lead to knots and ties in the old structure, which yield an incentive for more radical, structural change, as well as indications where to explore novel structure, in 'accommodation'.

This operationalises Hegel's dictum that 'in their failure one gets to know things', in his 'determinate negation'. Examples are Einstein's ideas of time and space, black holes, dark matter, electro-magnetism, and evolution as development without creation. I am reminded of Gaston Bachelard's view of 'philosophie du non', and Ganguilhem's claim of 'epistemological ruptures', which seem similar to Kuhn's later 'paradigm switches'. One can, under some conditions, say 'no' to current ideas. Adorno rejected such transcendence. The idea that ultimately an object can be fully covered by concepts without remainder, which Adorno calls 'identification', goes against Kant's dictum that we cannot know a thing 'as it is in itself'. I grant that one cannot be sure that failure will always yield transcendence. It depends on how fundamental and foundational the idea to be transcended is. Such ideas are often tacit, unconscious or taken as self-evident, deeply entrenched and beyond transformation.

I have elaborated the COD in terms of 'Scripts' [25]. A script is a network of 'nodes' that can be specialised activities in an overall structure. In a restaurant: entering, seating, ordering, eating, paying and leaving. Other scripts can be words in a sentence, variables in a mathematical proof, events in a narrative. A node has a repertoire of subscripts, such as forms of payment in the payment node of a restaurant script.

The model indicates two levels of change. One is incremental change, in a change of the subscript repertoire of a node, payment by telephone, say, in the payment node, and the second is radical change, of nodes and their order, as in the transformation to a self-service restaurant. This also affects the subscripts in nodes. In a self-service restaurant seating includes carrying a tray of food, in search of a table.

I propose that the COD is an example of what Derrida, 1930-2004, called 'deconstruction', and sometimes 'transformation', which entailed taking apart a system and then reconstructing it, often elsewhere. That is what the COD elaborates on. Derrida was on the way to a dynamic theory, but confusion arose about the term 'deconstruction'. My interpretation of deconstruction is that it attempts to reduce a proposition to its inevitable, often tacit, presuppositions. That is problematic, because if every proposition has presuppositions, how can one lay them bare if that also entails presuppositions? Derrida also offered the enigmatic notion of 'differance' (with an 'a'). That also evoked a variety of interpretations. It seems to mean the avoidance of precise and

---

25 Nooteboom, 2000

determinate meanings, allow for a diversity of meanings, thus allowing for a change of meanings. I opt for the interpretation of a never-ending process of making or encountering new, different meanings. This is reminiscent of the slogan 'imperfection on the move' of the philosophy blog that I run.

If those interpretations are somehow not 'legitimate' (what would be the criterion for that?), I make them to fit in my prejudgement of a dynamic perspective. As indicated for Foucault, for Derrida, and for the present book, this theory may be just as 'logocentrist' as the theories they condemn. However, I am not against logocentrism, rational reconstruction, because that is what theory is in the business of making, as long as it does not get stuck in statics, but studies their emergence, breakdown and transformation, and does not claim universal and unalterable truth. Some things are easier to theorise than others, such as poetry, love, truth, trust, democracy, happiness, etc. And a theory always has gaps and errors, and may be corrected and be developed in time.

About poetry it has been said, among other things, that rhythm derives from the thumping heart of a mother impacting on a foetus in the womb, or a galloping horse, but this is metaphor and does not explain much. Economies have been theorized from different perspectives, as I discuss elsewhere.

Schelling, 1775-1854, was also on the way to a dynamic theory of cognition and nature. Ideas arise from previous ideas, as nature arises from previous nature, in an unending process, in self-organisation, against the law of increasing entropy. Going against increasing entropy now even is a definition of life. He said: 'every new discovery throws us back into a new ignorance, and as one knot is untied, another is tied'[26] The latter is important because evolutionary epistemologists have been accused of going back to before Kant, assuming that there is a given, static 'selection environment'[27]. The nature that cognition adapts to is a moving target that may change faster than the cognition adapting to it. Schelling predated Derrida in rejoicing in difference. 'For Schelling thinking is the adventure of difference'[28]. He anticipated Kierkegaard, Nietzsche and Heidegger with his insistence of the 'finitude of reason'[29], and noted that 'authenticity means little more than concurrence with a recognizable group identity'.[30]

Why do all this striving without reaching perfection? Spinoza claimed that what we do is driven by an urge to survive, that he called 'conatus'. Plato claimed that people have an instinctive drive to manifest themselves ('thymos'). Thymos seems akin to the 'libidinal energies' that Lyotard saw absent from Marxism. Nietzsche spoke of a Dionysian orgiastic drive to live and express oneself, and proposed that this regularly goes against survival. I think it is an instinct arisen in evolution, because it yields discoveries that help survival, even if this misfires regularly.

---

26 Bowie,1993: 40
27 Bowie, 1993
28 Wirth, 2005: 4
29 Wirth, 2005: 13
30 Wirth, 2005: 15

Why or how do organisms and cells connect to achieve the benefits of a system, in self-organisation, against the law of increasing entropy? Of society we know that humans learned to collaborate, as conducive to group survival. In non-conscious nature we know of parasites and symbiosis, but how do the connections arise? Trees connect under the ground with their roots, connecting to threads of mycelium, in the exchange of sugars produced in the chlorophyl of their leaves, and minerals from the mycelium. In life, is there an inherent drive to connect, going against increasing entropy? Replacing Spinoza's 'conatus', I call this 'connectus'.

According to Edelman's 'Neural Darwinism' there is evolution also in the formation of the brain, where emerging neural networks compete for consolidation in adapting thresholds of firing[31], according to experienced success in understanding and the satisfaction of emotions.

Back to the COD. In its final stage, in consolidation, some obstacles may remain, in the new structure, which are gradually weeded out, though often not entirely. A novel script at the beginning carries along vestiges of the old one, yielding redundancy or inconsistency. Even later, there are remnants, yielding a layer of residues. Some innovations do not at the beginning flourish in the contexts they gradually conquer, and need at first to find niches where they can survive.

An example is the steam machine that was first used for pumping out water from a coal mine. Trains, factories

---

31 Edelman, 1987

and ships required ancillary innovations, such as pistons in the transfer of power to wheels. This is shown in some paintings of Turner, with lumbering steam ships alongside elegant sailing ships. A second example is a team of artillery that formerly was drawn by horses. The person shooting the cannon had to step back to control the horses from bolting at the boom. That stepping back was preserved when there no longer were horses.

The COD is an example of how in development discontinuity and continuity can alternate. Generalisation is continuous in its operation, accommodation is discontinuous, and this is preceded by reciprocation, which is something in between, keeping structure but modifying elements in them.

I go along with Adorno in taking an evolutionary view of reason[32]. In evolution, reason yielded the inhibition of impulse, needed for deliberation, favouring survival. It follows that later, when survival was assured, inhibitions could be released, forming part of present hedonism that seems to lead to ecological disaster. In the chapter on language, I will also take an evolutionary view. I do not, however, believe in teleology, the development towards an ultimate goal, as Hegel did.

What, then, is the sense of life? One gets a chance, in life, to make a contribution to society, in an attempt to make improvements in emancipation and freedom, without seeing it as a step towards some ultimate end.

In the human being, knowledge arises in a system of body and mind. A system has components, which together produce features that the system as a whole

---

32 O'Connor, 2013: 127

offers, but the components do not. That is called 'emergence'. For emergence, the components of the system need to be maintained within boundaries, in what is called 'homeostasis'. A human being has two connected areas of homeostasis, of body and mind. Bodily homeostasis applies for example to temperature, feeding, defecation, rest, blood flow, breathing and heartbeat. Merleau-Ponty called this intertwining of body and mind 'crossing' ('chiasm').[33]

As Damasio[34] explained, there is also psychological homeostasis in keeping mental states and emotions within bounds, in balances of intellect, emotions such as fear and impulse to run, impulse to fight, impulse to sex, anger, disgust, elation, reflexes, and they interact in a joint homeostasis with the body, and are constituted by parts of the brain and hormonal and neuronal processes. As a result of this, much mental activity is subconscious, and partly tacit. There is also a need for homeostasis on the level of society, where citizens and institutions move within constraints to contribute to the whole of the system. That seems to be crumbling, causing a threat to democracy.

I propose that the more or less tacit presuppositions of theory, which are difficult to deconstruct, are part of an epistemic homeostasis, to preserve what Gadamer called a 'tradition'.

For example, in the mind, the subconscious nature of thought is exhibited in so-called 'decision heuristics'. There are heuristics of 'loss aversion', exaggeration of

---

33 Merleau-Ponty, 1964.
34 2003

probability, 'escalation of commitment', and 'anchoring and adjustment'. The heuristic of loss aversion is that people will exert themselves more to avoid loss than to gain something. One can trace this to the condition in evolution that loss was often loss of life, which weighs more heavily than improvement of welfare.

In exaggeration of probability we jump to the conclusion that a phenomenon is recurring, which also had survival value in timely identification of a threat or opportunity. Escalation of commitment is increased commitment of resources in the case of loss, on the assertion that otherwise the loss would have been in vain. Anchoring and adjustment means that one sticks to a failing arrangement and engages only in marginal changes to it, while it failure is more radical, and more drastic change is required. Pervasive subconscious procedures are routines that were once deliberated but have become automatic, which is beneficial in opening capacity for deliberation concerning new experience.

A system can change, but slowly, in changing its elements and their connections while maintaining homeostasis. Development of a system can peter out, in a dead end. However, in the history of thought there are many examples of thought escaping from a dead end.

Examples are the escape from Newton's thought into that of Einstein, the escape from phlogiston theory, from the earth as centre of the universe, from divine creation of the world, and so on. They are not sudden turnarounds, but slow transformations, where the initiator is ostracised, often till after his death.

A tenacious intellectual habit is for people to try to categorise things, objects and people, i.e. put them into conceptual boxes; the identification Adorno militated against. It is inevitable because that gives a handle on things, which we need to manipulate to maintain life, but it violates the idea that the object is to be understood in interaction with the subject, and is not that perspicuous, always hides part of itself, has an unknown potential to manifest itself in ways we don't know. Adorno recognised the need for 'non-coercive identification', which recognises its limitation, and is tentative, preliminary. This rhymes with the principle of 'imperfection on the move' that I have been advocating (see my philosophy blog of that name: 'philosophyonthemove.blogspot.nl'). We never achieve perfection, but that is no reason not to strive for improvement, even if the result is still imperfect. Central to Continental philosophy is the idea that coercive categorisation does not do justice either to the world or to humanity.

Homeostasis of society is achieved by moral and ethical principles, such as containment of violence, empathy, loyalty, love, friendship, with social norms, and the virtues of commitment, courage, moderation, and justice.

Horkheimer and Adorno emphasised the inhibitory side of society, reducing people to their roles in the system, but they seemed to undervalue the positive side of the system of lifting so many people out of enslaving poverty. Society does yield a tension between the urge for authenticity and the need for conformity, to which I will return.

In contrast with many Continental Philosophers, I do not reject science. I have been a scientist myself, testing hypothesis in econometric models of economic phenomena. However, I grant the limits and the captivity of science to background assumptions lingering from evolution. Scientific theories are based on assumptions, explicit or tacit, that are not themselves amenable to scientific testing, and are a matter of taste, aesthetics or tradition, and in their analysis lies the task of philosophy. It has been called 'pre-science'[35]. I employ science not as a universal method, but as yielding some interesting insights, such as those of evolution, brain science, psychology, and sociology. For example, science of the brain shows how reason is intertwined with emotions and routines, which are largely subconscious.

In the discussion of science, I follow the view of Lakatos[36], that scientific disciplines, or what Lakatos called 'research programmes', have a 'hard core' of fundamental assumptions that are kept immune from falsification, protected by a 'protective belt' of auxiliary assumptions that may be adapted to divert any falsification. This is reminiscent of Gadamer's notion of scientist following a 'tradition'. Not all practitioners in the research programme or tradition may be aware of its origins, and even among its historians there may be lacunae and disgreement.

This is a form of conservatism that goes against Popper's rule that scientists should seek falsification. In a

---

35 Critchley, 2001: 116
36 1978

famous debate[37], Feyerabend retorted that this is not what scientists in fact do. For their career and prestige, they prefer to find confirmations, and leave falsification to competing colleagues, and Popper finally conceded that it may be rational to accumulate falsifications, with maintenance of the core, to 'find out where the real strengths of a theory lie'. This indicates the rationality of a certain 'theoretical conservatism' in 'programme continuity'.

As a result, scientists who do not belong to the community that huddles in the hard core, certainly if they criticise it, will be barred from the book series and journals that the members of that community edit, in their roles of editors and reviewers, as 'gate keepers'. Thus, to break into established areas with their entrenched programmes, emerging scientists often had to institute their own journals and books. Examples in economics are the 'Journal of Evolutionary Economics', 'The Journal of Institutional Economics', and the 'Journal of Trust Research'. These all deviate from the core methodological rule that economists should maximise an objective function, in an equilibrium of supply and demand. Evolutionary economists argue that in economies equilibria are seldom reached. Institutional economists argue that there may be other goals than maximum profit. Mainstream economists look down on trust because it is partly non-rational. I discuss this theory of research programmes, because it is a vivid example of Adorno's view that collective thought may thwart individual expression and development.

---

37 Lakatos and Musgrave, 1970

This is an example of what Rorty called 'language games of different communities'. The example qualifies Rorty's claim that science creates 'solidarity' between scientists. It also shows how within such communities there indeed is such solidarity, despite rivalry. Debate and agreement arise, on the basis of mutually agreed facts and explanatory principles.

I maintain the notion of truth as 'warranted assertability' proposed by John Dewey, in which practical usefulness and origin of a claim play a role. Admittedly, that is a social practice. There is no universal but only local objectivity, within the game. Gadamer proposed a similar principle, which yields not a scientific demonstration , but a persuasive argumentation.[38] Contrary to Rorty, literature is less justified than such argumentation. Fiction authors do not vie for justification (but they may compete for prizes), as scholars do, and they construe their own personal worlds.

If Rorty is right, with his language games, how can I claim to connect different language games? Different Lakatosian research programmes have different 'hard cores' that cannot be reconciled, but nevertheless they often have much in common, which may be used to connect them, in trying to trigger mutual understanding. But, due to the incommensurability of hard cores, one would have to construct a new language game. In economics I did that with studies on innovation and evolution, which got me a prize from the 'International Joseph E Schumpeter Society'. In political economy it got me the 'Gunnar Myrdal prize' for analysing trust as a process.

---

38 Madison, 1992: 321

In the present book I construct a dynamic view of knowledge on the basis of the COD, of language on the basis of the Hermeneutic Circle, of ethics in the development of 'phronesis', and in the study of societal evolution.

Concerning the COD, from a discussion with a former CEO of a large oil company, I learned how at first foreign operations had to stick to established practice from the home country, to profit from the higher efficiency of large volumes, which would be affected by mingling with local practice, until they saw that it promotes innovation, which could have priority over efficiency, but it was a struggle to change the ruling mind-frame. There is a cumulative effect in reciprocation: as experience with it increases, one increases the 'absorptive capacity' of assimilating what is foreign.

The COD also informs personal communication. One may see it as 'generalisation', where one tries to fit one's thoughts or practices into the cognitive framework of the other, and vice versa. This is an elaboration of Habermas's communicative action and Gadamer's view of communication. If that does not work, one can say or show it differently, tapping from experience, and when that does not work, one can accommodate to the other, trying to change one's thought to assimilate his. One would like to see more of that in the debate between AP and CP. This is what reciprocity demands and offers, in the attempt at understanding. Such communication across boundaries of language games is aided by metaphor, where one tries to elucidate one's thinking in terms of the other's parlance.

There is what I call 'cognitive distance'; differences between people in understanding. In communication, one has to cross that distance, and shorter distance allows for easier understanding , but larger distance promises more novelty. Thus, one must seek a distance that is large enough to yield novelty, but not too large to block understanding, in what might be called 'optimal distance'. This is not known beforehand, and requires trial and error. It can yield a widening or shift of perspective.

This also applies on the level of organisations and culture. It is a task of leadership or government to nourish mutual difference for novelty in accommodation, as well as sufficient mutual understanding. I call this 'organisational focus', with a shared purpose, operating producers, mutual understanding and cooperation, not to have to negotiate everything at each turn.

How narrow or tight the focus should be depends on the purpose of the organisation. If the prime purpose is efficient production, the penalty on lack of understanding and agreement is high, and the focus should be relatively narrow. When the purpose is innovation, which requires variety, the focus needs to be relatively wide.

How is an appropriate focus achieved? Here lies the possibly highest task of management. The focus is supported by organisational culture, reporting procedures, office rituals, parties, decorations, interior design, self-selection and socialisation of newcomers. This yields a narrowing of perspective, to some extent, because of which one has to entertain collaborative relations with other organisations with a different focus, not to miss out too much on opportunities and fail to see threats.

Can focus change? It should develop as conditions change. It can change by external criticism, by shareholders or society, as now in the need for adequate environmental policy. There can be internal criticism, but this has the risk of derailing the organisation's need for focus. What is truth? I do not believe in the old 'correspondence theory', according to which concepts correspond to things in reality. Vico acknowledged that mathematics is the paragon of truth, but only because we have made it. It is certain only in its derivation from axioms that we have thought up, and different axioms will yield different deductions. The other basis for scientism is empirical testing, but facts can be problematic because they are 'loaded' with theory. This undermines empiricism. However, this can be exaggerated. The theory locked up in facts is wider than the theories at issue. Economists and Sociologists are at odds over, say the causes of unemployment, while agreeing on the statistics of it.

I adopt a pragmatic stance, with Dewey's notion of 'warranted assertability', where something is considered true when supported by facts, logic, theory, practical usefulness, and its origin, Gadamer's 'tradition'. Origins cannot, however, be fully traced, and remain partly hidden.

Does truth depend on power? Since truth is judged on argument, it is social, and yes: acceptance of argument depends on power, both negative, when it enforces agreement, and positive, when it yields insight. CP philosophers (Adorno, Lyotard) emphasise the negative side. Such power often gets institutionalised, as, for example in science, where theoretical perspectives become dogma, and you are ostracised when not adhering to it, as used to happen in religion. The neo-liberal ideology of markets has brought prosperity, but also a destruction of sociality in economics. If you do not comply, what you propose must therefore be nonsense. I was critical of economics, and not just ostracised, but seen as a deviant, even a traitor. Once I submitted an article to a journal, and it was rejected with the verdict that 'this article does not maximise an objective function under side conditions, therefore it is not science'. Foucault[39] attributed such regimentation to social science in general, and more specifically, to disciplines of care, schooling and organisation.

My criticism of all this is as follows. One may not like it, but how else is society to be coordinated, if not by some sort of homeostasis, by authority and some discipline? It may be more or less suppressive, but it is also inevitable, in some form.

In its mission to eliminate myth and superstition, the Enlightenment led to measurement as a canon of rationality[40]. Take economics. The central method of mainstream economics was to maximise a function of utility. This requires measurement of utility. The first attempt was to assign numbers to alternatives, but the problem turned out to be that it is not credible to claim that choices can be made on a single dimension. Can you compare the smile of your daughter with the delight of an ice-cream, and of listening to your favourite music? The next move was to do no more than ranking preferences: A>B>C. But one can have one ordering on one

---

39 Foucault, 1994
40 Horkheimer and Adorno, 1968

dimension, say price, and another on quality, say: C>A>B. Better quality is often more expensive, and you may find it hard to choose between the two. What to do? You may discuss the choice, and bring up further dimensions to consider. Often, choices are made impulsively, or intuitively, like buying a car on the ground of its looks, perhaps on the design of its outside mirror. Advertising exploits such impulse, presenting a car with an attractive female figure, or in an exciting seaboard ride, to make it alluring, appealing to unconscious desire.

Another example is the measurement of publication performance at universities. The practice now is measurement of the number of publications, weighted with the 'citation score' i.e. the average number of times an article in the journal is cited, which often discounts books, for which citation scores are scarce, while in some disciplines, such as philosophy, books are primary. Also, there arise 'citation circles', where friends cite each other without reading their work. That is be expected. Regulations call forth evasion. This is not to say that one should not measure, but that one should see how it can flatten issues, or can 'reify' them, to use such that expression of Adorno's.

The unknown, outside turbulence is threatening. Then one can do two things. One is to keep it out. An example is economics, which takes flight in the notion of risk in contrast with uncertainty. In risk one does not know what will happen, but one does know what *can* happen, one attaches probabilities, and calculates the best course of action. Economists avoid uncertainty, not knowing all that can happen, because then one cannot calculate utility, and as a result do not treat innovation adequately. One often does not know all that can happen. Another way to keep uncertainty out is myth, and science plays that role to some extent, of pretending we have it under control. From a prejudicial perspective, many people want to keep refugees out, but one can also welcome them inside, as much as possible.

A fundamentally different response is to bring the uncertain inside, and welcome it. That is what the Taoist does: uncertainty, unpredictability, calamity and human fallacy are inherent in the nature of the world, resist all our efforts of control, and should yet be embraced as inevitable, and one should become resilient to them. Death is part of life. Nietzsche also had this idea of flux, development, genealogy, of morality and customs, as haphazard, contingent, unpredictable and uncontrollable. Resilience is also preached by Stoicism.

This is also reminiscent of Kierkegaard, who also pleaded for resilience in adversity. One should not surrender to a position of victim to circumstances. That is a violation of good faith, and a sin against spirit. Circumstances may determine *what* one chooses, not *that* one chooses. De Key quotes a saying of Simone de Beauvoir: De resistance of the environment supports the action of Man (freedom), as the air supports the flight of a bird.[41]

A question in CP is that people are not and should not be treated as the same. Among other things, they can't have identical knowledge. That would require the same inherited intelligence, education and experience, yielding the

---

41   De Key 1975: 152.

background knowledge they have acquired and developed. That yields a difference that is part of what Lyotard called 'le differend'.

It is difficult to drop all what I call the 'object bias', seeing abstract things as objects, and this has caused untold confusion in philosophy. We saw things as marbles, and now we have lost our marbles. A social or linguistic structure is seen as a machine with fixed parts, without freedom, while it is more like a can of worms. A whole stream of especially French Continental philosophers, such as Lyotard, Foucault, Derrida and Rorty, have militated against 'structuralism', with authoritarian regimes that erase or disregard differences, and suffocate freedom for the sake of the whole of the system, as in the philosophy of Hegel. I propose that he challenge is to conceptualise systems with as much freedom as possible for the parts and transforming partly because of it. This is an issue also in organisation studies.

The conclusions of this chapter are as follows: First, knowledge is a process rather than a possession or state; a process of interaction between subject and object that can yield advance but never perfection. 'Advance' can be increase of prosperity, emancipation, safety, justice, satisfaction, spirituality. Advance usually requires generalisation of current knowledge or practice into a new context where one runs into their limits, and acquires incentives from failure and opportunities for novel elements, from local knowledge and practice. Vico preluded on the dynamic nature of knowledge, saying 'We can be said to know a thing if we know why it is as it is, or how it came to be, or was made to be'[42].

A second conclusion is, that the acquisition of knowledge requires interaction between people at some 'cognitive distance', which requires and develops 'absorptive capacity' for novelty. One needs opposition from the other to become oneself.

A third conclusion is that uncertainty should not be fled from but embraced.

---

42   Berlin, 2013: 39.

Language

As Gadamer argued, language and thought are constitutive of each other, both carry a bias and are temporary. It is conceivable that there is mental activity and communication without language, as in emotional response and body language, but they would be very primitive. The challenge is to devise a theory of language that on the one hand yields a shared, sufficiently stable meaning of words to enable communication, and on the other hand allows for shifting personal associations and memories, which inject variety, individuality and change of meaning.

This fits with the endeavour, in CP, at 'understanding' rather than deductive explanation, with insight in the 'genealogy', the process of the development of meanings, and the process of interaction between the self and the others, between context and text, in the 'hermeneutic circle'. This is illustrated in figure 3. A new context has the potential to shift our understanding, and a new understanding can create new contexts, and makes us look differently at the world.

Figure 3 hermeneutic circle

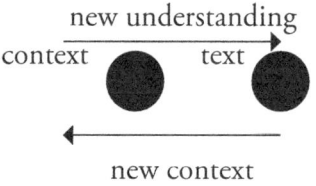

This is consonant with the 'cycle of discovery' (COD) derived from Jean Piaget, discussed in the chapter on knowledge. That can be seen as an elaboration of the hermeneutic circle, showing how one can get from a change of context to a new understanding, and from there to a change of content.

Frege is usually seen as a prime analytic philosopher, but his ideas can contribute to the understanding of hermeneutics. He distinguished between 'reference' and 'sense'[43]. In reference we aim to refer to something in the world. Sense is 'the way in which something manifests itself' (*die Art des Gegebenseins*), as Frege put it. The classic example of sense is Venus, which is seen as the 'morning star' as well as the 'evening star', depending on when it is seen.

I would interpret it somewhat differently. Since we do not know reality as it is in itself, or we do not know in what sense and to what extent we do, we cannot call reference actual, but only intentional: we aim to refer, in the practical conduct of life and communication. I would call sense 'the way in which we identify things', as a morning or evening star, for example. It is subjective, part of personal experience, and unstable, as people build up their frames of mind, through a sequence of experiences. It is the 'interpretative' side of meaning, loaded with emotions and morality.

Ferdinand de Saussure[44] distinguished between 'langue', the intersubjective, stable, synchronous meaning of a

---

43 Frege, 1892; Thiel, 2013
44 1979

word, and grammar, at a given time, and 'parole', the diachronous, fluid, personal memories and associations attached to a word or expression, which change in time and occasionally can cause 'langue' to shift. Langue makes for the unity of language (Saussure, 1979: 270), and parole for its diversity. If personal meaning becomes widely shared, parole shifts langue, to some extent. Intentional reference is langue, and parole is sense. However, even langue is subject to shifts. In Saussure's words, 'The river of langue streams without interruption' (p. 192), but 'Nothing enters langue without having been tried in parole, and all evolutionary phenomena have their roots in the sphere of the individual'(p.231). Saussure focussed on langue, discussing phonology, for example, but I am primarily interested in parole, as the source of the dynamics of meaning.

De Saussure used the notion of 'syntagma', a string of words, expressing a concrete account of something. It belongs to parole, unless it is a fixed expression, such as 'throwing a look', or 'throwing in the towel'. Then, being fixed, it belongs to langue.[45] Conversely, public items of langue can be given idiosyncratic, deviant connotations, in poetry especially, for example the word 'storm' for a conflict.

For another example, take Covid, or Corona. Everybody knows its meaning, in langue, of being a contagious virus, for which there is a vaccine. In parole, meaning picks up personal experience with it, oneself and among family and friends, one's assessment of the risk of getting contaminated, one's opinion on the measures taken by

---

45 Saussure, 1979: 172

the government, such as lockdown and distancing, one's willingness to get vaccinated, and one's confidence in the vaccine.

Spoken language preceded writing, in calling out to warn, attract, locate and collaborate. In ancient Egypt writing was a collection of pictures as symbols of people, gods and events, in Russia it was Cyrillic script. In Western Europe lower case letters were invented next to capitals, next came the printing press, and digitalisation and Internet. That has created a new world, as in social media, guided by algorithms. There now is fear that in 'ChatGPT', algorithms will overwhelm us.

Language yields and requires communication, mutual interpretation and understanding, in what earlier, in the chapter on knowledge, following Piaget, I called 'assimilation'.

Schleiermacher, 1768-1834, distinguished between 'grammatical' and 'psychological' hermeneutics. The first is systematic, coherent and logical, the second 'psychological', with empathy and what Schleiermacher called 'psychological divination', with empathy and identification.[46] Here I connect that with the distinction between reference and sense, and between langue and parole.

In communication, people look at each other and often smile, in contrast with animals, who look away and are frightened at the baring of teeth. Regards and facial expressions help to convey intentions, help to express parole. If telecommunication is not conducted with facetime, and people don't look at each other, communication

---

46 Sherrat, 2006: 61.

breaks loose, and transgresses especially moral limits, exploding in infective and threats. The latest development in AI is that of 'Chat-GPT", which produces texts that can be difficult to distinguish from human texts. It lacks parole, because parole is based on experience along a path of life, with unexpected, unpredictable experiences. Chat-GPT is crammed with human texts that its algorithms rearrange to answer a query, but has no 'personal' experience. Can this be called experience? Can a mix of parole from different people be said to achieve parole on the basis of the experience of many people? Can sense-mixing yield sense-making? If you mix beans you don't get a bean. However, in time robots may develop experience that yields parole.

Uprooting established meanings in langue occurs especially in poetry, when it replaces or shifts meaning by unleashing parole, supported by metaphor and aided by rhyme and rhythm. To compare a relation to a storm indicates its upheaval, with leaves of words being torn from branches of reason, but also that it can subside, and let the sun shine again. Visual art can also yield new perspectives. Art has been conceived as 'mimesis', imitation, also by Horkheimer and Adorno. It was that, in realist painting such as still life and portraits, but now, in non-figurative art, I propose, it trains and primes the mind for the horizontal transcendence Adorno argues for. Adorno lauded art for escaping from the obsession with efficiency, instrumental rationality, and giving room for the intrinsic value of the life world.

This does not mean that there is no representation in art. There can be representation without imitation. An example dissected by Adorno is the work of Franz Kafka. Kafka did not describe society in established terms, but revealed its hidden irrationalities, erratics, injustices, absurdities, and thus adhered to the notion presented here of art as transcending established views. Is there a limit? When does mimesis turn into transcendence? In the chapter on knowledge I discussed degrees of innovation, incremental innovation that is still 'assimilation', integrating new elements in an existing structure, and 'radical' innovation or 'accommodation' that changes structure. Here, what I am trying to say, is that art prompts accommodation. Sometimes, inventors talk poetry.

How about musicians, dancers, or other performers, and their audiences? In French, performance is 'interpretation', which performers achieve every time anew. Interpretation goes beyond formulas and routines. It is not entertainment, and does not appeal to daily experience. Audiences may be lifted out of their experience of identity. All this is literally 'ecstasy'. It appeals to parole rather than langue, to accommodation rather than assimilation. Whatever it is, it is akin to, or ancillary to, the horizontal transcendence I discussed before.

How does meaning change? The 'hermeneutic circle' [47] is a model of the dynamics of meaning that results from the interplay of langue and parole. On a vertical 'paradigmatic axis' lie abstract, general, public, universal concepts, in langue, and the order of grammatical rules. On the horizontal, 'syntagmatic axis', they are brought together, where the context, with different

---

47 Gadamer, 2008

words bumping into each other, evokes individual cases from universals, which carry along personal associations and recollections, in parole. The idea of a fossilised, formal, public, mostly written language in distinction with a living language, spoken language, is an old one, going back to Vico and Herder, for example[48].

As I said in the chapter on knowledge, people have different cognitive frames, which yield what I earlier called 'cognitive distance'. In communication one must try to 'cross' that distance , by assimilating what another says and does, and, if that does not succeed, to accommodate one's mind frames to them. In communication, one should seek to connect to the other's parole, appealing to what is familiar to the other, what he can assimilate. This requires openness, dedication and effort. One can help the other to accommodate by using metaphors, trying to explain one's thought in the language of the other. This requires that in communication one should try to connect to the other's sense, parole. Perhaps, pace Habermas, one can say that parole is the attempt at expressing the 'life world'.

Government actions are necessarily technocratic to a large extent, but that is not the basis for communicating it to the citizen. Genuine communication should connect with the 'lifeworld' of the people, making 'sense' to them, in 'communicative interaction' that should be free of authoritarian imposition ('Herrschaftsfrei'; Habermas,1982). Lyotard claimed that consensus is an illusion, hiding the dominance of one interlocutor over another.

---

48 Berlin, 1976

There is no universal history. A history is always that of the victor, neglecting or excluding the underdog.

Usually, with 'communication' we intend to refer to positive exchange of information, enlightenment, explanation, and so on, but it has a negative side of misunderstanding, obfuscation, confusion, suppression, manipulation, jargon, excess nuance, lies, false promises, twisting facts, saying the obvious, and illocution. Politicians are prone to do this, to circumvent criticism or inability, or to procrastinate. Perhaps we should add to the definition that communication should be dialogical, reciprocal, or what Adorno called 'intermediation', in Buber's I-Thou relations that I will discuss later.

'Illocution' is intended not so much to inform but to 'make people do things'[49], like a command or inducement, or 'performative', like declaring that a meeting is opened, expression of endearment, or excuse. It is a legitimate form of communication, but can derail in distraction and manipulation.

In studies of communication, Eduard Hall [50] made a distinction between 'low context' communication with precise, explicit, logical, public, coherent use of words, and 'high context' communication, which is ambiguous, context-dependent, personal, using body language, expression, relying on trust, and aimed at maintaining the relation concerned.[51] I relate this to Saussure's distinction between langue and parole, Frege's distinction between reference and sense, and Martin Buber's distinction

---

49 Austin,1955; Searle, 1969
50 1967
51 Ramos, 2014

between 'I-it' and 'I-Thou' relations[52]. The former are extrinsic, instrumental, self-interested, one-directional, or what Adorno called 'reified'. The latter are intrinsic, reciprocal, bi-directional, and are called 'mediation' by Adorno, as part of what he called 'understanding' ('verstehen'). Adorno's view that art is not part of instrumental reason then suggests that there is art in I-Thou relations.

This is what distinguishes CP most from AP, I think. I will return to Buber in the chapter on ethics.

It is an illusion to think that I-Thou relations are free of power, but if that is negative power, the relation is not what Buber intended for such relationships. There, power should be mostly positive, enabling. Sense, parole, high context, and I-Thou express the humanism in CP.

Can one make language? No and yes. The development of language is a collective, not an individual affair, so: No: there is no private language. But individuals, often public figures, such as politicians, columnists, popular writers, artists, or song writers, can voice new notions or meanings of existing notions that catch on in public usage, so: Yes. They can arise from parole, to become part of langue, or, in terms of the hermeneutic circle, arise from the syntagmatic axis and become part of the paradigmatic axis. In listening or reading, parole crops up and colours interpretation, as Gadamer argued.

How has language evolved, and what are the consequences? As concerning reason, concerning language I also take an evolutionary approach. According to

---
52 Buber, 2004

Tomassello [53] and Moseley[54], language developed from the times that the human being was a hunter-gatherer, and language was needed for collaboration, in hunting and defence, and these required an adequate conceptualisation of things moving in time and space, such as a running prey, an approaching enemy, an incoming spear, a lost baby, the location of shelter. I call this the 'object bias'. Vico already preluded on this.[55] The evolutionary approach tells us that in the debate on realism, conceptualisation must have some adequacy to the world, or the human being would not have survived.

According to Lakoff and Johnson [56] we conceptualise abstraction on the basis of metaphor to objects in time and space. One is the 'container metaphor', such as being 'in' love, 'in order', 'at' war, etc. 'Going up' is a metaphor for things going well, such as economic growth or profits, because one is upright when well, prostate when being ill or dead.

I call this metaphoric language an 'object bias'. This conceptualisation in terms of objects in time and space is not appropriate for abstract concepts such as identity, happiness, democracy, meaning, communication etc. that matter in present evolution. Nationality is not like being in some box, since one can have different nationalities at a time. Communication is not like shipping the meaning of a word as an item in a communication channel. In transferring a word from one sentence to another,

---

53 2016
54 2019
55 Berlin, 2013: 54
56 1980

its meaning changes, it is as if being carried from one room to another, a chair drops a leg or changes colour. Our early mind treated things as marbles, and in modern times we have lost our marbles.

It is difficult to drop the object bias, and this has caused untold confusion in philosophy. A social or linguistic structure was seen as a machine with fixed parts, without freedom, while it is more like a can of worms. A whole stream of especially French Continental philosophers, such as Lyotard, Foucault, Derrida and Rorty (American), have militated against 'structuralism', with things being part of a hole, yielding authoritarian regimes that erase or disregard differences, and suffocate freedom for the sake of the whole of the system, as in the philosophy of Hegel. The object bias, I propose, yields what Foucault called 'presence', and militated against.

The challenge is to conceptualise systems with as much freedom as possible for the parts, and more fluidity. This is an issue also in organisation studies. We need a notion of identity as not being fixed, but developing, with numerous, mostly forgotten and imagined connections.

Can different words have equal meaning? That would require equal langue and equal parole, and the latter raises the question 'for whom' and 'when?'.

A conclusion of this chapter is that the 'hermeneutic circle' can be elucidated with the 'Cycle of Discovery', where assimilation develops into accommodation. A second conclusion is that there are two dimensions to language: A set of synchronic, public, stable, shared meanings, called 'langue', and a variety of diachronic, personal meanings, pregnant with individual meanings, called 'parole'. A third conclusion is that language has evolved with an 'object bias' that conceives of abstract notions as metaphors to objects in time and space. The good news is that in every-day life, such concepts are reasonably realistic, or else humanity would not have survived in evolution, but the bad news is that our conceptualisation of abstractions is faulty.

Ethics

A central issue in society is the relation between self and other. Can there be equality? For people to be equal, they would have to share inherited potential and identical paths of life, and that does not apply even to co-eval twins.

Relations between people depend on one's ethical view. In Western cultures, the four dominant ethical systems are utility ethics, which dominates economics and present Western society, duty ethics or 'deontology' (the classical Greek word for duty is 'deon'), and 'virtue ethics'. I adopt virtue ethics, and will discuss it here. It largely goes back to Aristotle, was lost out of sight for a while, and reappeared around 1950[57]. A fourth vision of the good life is that of Stoicism, which also goes back to the ancient Greeks and Romans, with Seneca and Roman emperor Marcus Aurelius as prominent adherents. For the Stoic, one must follow the order of nature, and exercise the reason that is given to the human being. The nature of the human being includes sociality, in dedication to others and shared interest, with a feeling for fairness and justice. For Seneca, the practice of reason is the only thing that contributes to the good life. All else, such as riches and health, lies outside happiness. While Aristotle granted that material things contribute to the good life, the stoic rejects it. One may enjoy them, as long as they do not

---

57 Hursthouse, 1999; Snow, 2020

obstruct the virtue of reason[58]. The Christian church has amply borrowed from stoicism[59].

My understanding of a virtue is that it is a more or less stable inclination towards a practice that one believes to contribute to the good life of self and other. In Aristotle's view, the good life is that of a reasonable, social and political being. oriented at the community.[60]

One stream in virtue ethics is oriented at the good life and concerns the question 'why' one would enact virtues. Other factors than virtues also contribute to the good life, such as health and happiness. Criticism has arisen against eudaimonic ethics that it is too much oriented to the self, though Aristotle did not aim at self-interest, but at what is good for the community. Modern forms of virtue ethics developed that take into account the wellbeing of others, in empathy, benevolence and care.

A second stream of virtue ethics is oriented at the intention of the actor. Positive inclinations are reason, courage, empathy, moderation and justice. Negative inclinations are lying, cruelty, hatred, jealousy. Here, motivation is more important than outcomes, because one can do good and bad things by accident. It is about the 'how' of action[61].

The work of Francis Hutcheson belongs to this stream[62]. It also had a streak of utilitarianism, by attaching value to the highest happiness of the greatest number

---

58   Annas, 2006: 156, 160
59   Welchman, 2006a: 41
60   Swanton, 2013
61   Welchman, 2006a: ix
62   Hutcheson, 2006

of people, but if that is achieved by self-interest, it does not count.

In a third stream of virtue ethics the question is central whether an action 'achieves its goal'. Outcomes matter. This concerns 'what' one should do[63]. Christine Swanton [64] also shifted the focus away from motivation. She grants that goal achievement is seldom perfect. One can enact a virtue too little or too much. Taking into account others can derail in self-sacrifice, and courage can derail in recklessness. This recalls Aristotle's seeking of the 'middle'. Especially when judging whether a virtue achieves its purpose, one should consider the conditions. This brings us to 'phronesis'.

Aristotelian ethics was not so much based on universal rules, applying always to everyone, but on principles of action that are individualised according to the conditions at hand. In 'phronesis', the highest virtue, sometimes one is indulgent, sometimes rigorous and principled. Some people are virtuosos in this balancing, and can serve as role models.

The body is flexible. Negt and Kluge, [65]showed the versatility of our hands and fingers, with a hard grip, as on a hammer, a hand brake, a pump, etc., and a soft, delicate grip, on a needle for sewing, picking up a pebble, raising a cup of tea, buttoning a shirt, and a range of body language, facial expressions, such as growls, smiles, knitted and raised eyebrows, stares, and tones of voice. That versatility has developed in evolution. We need a similar

---

63 Welchman, 2006a: ix
64 2001
65 2014

range of phronesis, with a tight and a soft grip, in negotiating virtues. Phronesis should use the full potential of body language, facial expressions, and tone of voice, in observing virtues and expressing them. Will further evolution develop that in time, or will humanity destroy itself before that time? Phronesis should also spy for the parole behind langue; the song of it, the tragedy of it, the resonance of it.

Deviating from universals is a tricky move. If rules are too lax, they have no bite, and open the door to special pleading, cronyism and corruption. Though virtues are seldom universal, there are universal vices, such as murder, torture, and knowingly condemning an innocent person, and in that Aristotelian ethics is somewhat deontic[66].

The distinction between the universal and the particular is too stark. Some principles are so general as to allow for few exceptions, approaching, but not quite achieving, universality, leaving room sometimes for special cases. In war, under attack, if necessary to defend oneself, as now in Ukraine, one may kill

Though Aristotle denied it, in some circumstances virtues can come into conflict with each other, as when honesty and empathy can conflict, in the white lie to a hostess that her dinner was superb, while you found it inedible, or lie to soothe your child in danger. People often find it difficult to combine the virtues of honesty and solidarity with self-interest, as in policies taken to fight Covid-19.

---

66 Snow, 2018

The three streams of virtue ethics are complementary rather than being rivals.[67] Often, some utilitarianism sneaks into virtue ethics, in attention to the outcome of an intendedly virtuous act. A virtue is seldom perfectly enacted. Next to a good life as a goal, often more myopic motives sneak in, and according to Aristoteles, that is all right, up to a point, as long as it is remains within bounds and does not derail into a blind craving.

Is the enactment of virtues instinctive, intuitive or rational? It is all of those. Instinct is an inheritance from evolution. Intuition is subconscious, tacit, impulsive, automatic, based on experience, turning thoughts and actions into routine. Adorno worried that if morality is rational, it can be overruled by reason, in political expedience, as when Nazism led to the holocaust, and Putin caused the current horrors in Ukraine. Adorno pleaded for impulse as the driver of action. The problem with that is. that it could also yield brutal personal vengeance or aggression. There should be a balance of instinct, intuition and reason, in phronesis.

Kierkegaard proposed a personal ethic that trumps virtues and morality, and for him it is connected to religion, and this developed into the relation with the other, who has the 'face of God', as Levinas put it.

What virtues are at issue? The foremost 'cardinal' virtues, around which much turns, are reason, courage, constraint, and justice. There are secondary virtues, such as hospitality, sincerity, truthfulness, resilience, empathy, and even humour (already mentioned by Aristotle). Christian religion adds: love, hope and fidelity. I add trust.

---

67 Swanton, 2003

The virtue of Phronesis is needed to deal with dilemma's, and life is full of them[68]. We may not be aware of them, we may try to ignore them, avoid them, or we may find them interesting, enlightening, and even useful. We may create them, in imposing a threat of punishment, telling a child to return a stolen toy or else ….Think of Solomon's judgement in threatening to cut a contested baby in half, in order to find out who the real mother is, who prefers to surrender the baby to the surrogate mother over having it killed. A dilemma is not just a comparison, it calls for a choice. Is the dilemma productive, in generating a synthesis, or is it just a bothersome enigma? One can choose one of the opposites of the dilemma, alternate between them, depending on the circumstances, one can take a middle position, and in *dialectics* one combines thesis and antithesis in a *synthesis*.

Old Chinese philosophy (in particular Taoism) opposes dichotomies, such as true versus untrue, between which you have to choose, and sees them as polarities, where you can choose a position in between. From one perspective you lean towards one side, from another perspective to the other side. To understand one side you need to know the other side. Perhaps one should accept that dilemmas cannot always be resolved, and are to be accepted as an inevitable part of life, indeed as a challenge that constitutes the gist of life, precisely in trying but failing to resolve them.

According to Darnell et al, phronesis has two functions: constitutive and integrative. In the constitutive function one appreciates the salient factors of a given

---

68 Wall, 2003

situation, in the integrative function one brings those factors together to arrive at a balance, on the basis of the vision of who one wants to be. Darnell et al[69] call this the 'Blueprint' for the good life. Martha Nussbaum[70] indicated that literature offers an exercise in 'moral perception', phantasy and sensitivity needed for a full moral life, with attention to vulnerability, obstinacy, accidents and variability, 'fragility' of the human condition, as Nussbaum called it.

The second model discussed by Darnell et.al. is developed on the basis of earlier work by Kohlberg. The four facets are here: moral sensitivity, moral judgment, moral motivation implementation. Moral sensitivity concerns the effect of action on others. Moral judgment concerns reasoning, implementation concerns character, and social, and psychological skills.

The two models in fact much resemble each other. Both have the rational balance of moral principles, character and properties and emotions of involvement. However, in the second model circumstances are hardly taken into account. In both models we recognise the three streams in the literature on virtue ethics: The 'why' of the good life, 'we' as the person one wants to be, the 'how' of the capabilities of the actor, and the 'what' of effects of action, goal achievement.

Morality can go too far. Plato gave the image of reason as a charioteer, controlling two wild horses: eros, desire, including desire for knowledge, and 'thymos', the urge to manifest oneself. Spinoza later claimed that people are

---
69 2019: 34
70 2001

driven by 'conatus', an urge to act and survive. Thymos is not only vanity, urge for reputation, as Fukuyama[71] claimed. It is also the drive of entrepreneurs, discoverers, researchers and politicians to achieve something new, to 'make a difference', and that is also a virtue. Nietzsche championed thymos. He rebelled against morality[72]. He exalted the will to power, which originally led to overpowering others, but developed into the joy of removing obstacles. He saw morality as the revenge and protection of the weak person, with a 'slave mentality', in opposition to the strong. He appreciated Apollo, the god of harmony, but his heart lay with Dionysus, the god of chaos and drunkenness, the god who dances with mavericks. He argued against equality, and wanted a ranking of people according to achievement and excellence. One finds such ranking everywhere: in sports, entertainment, theatre, science, business and politics. To say that everyone is to be treated equally, is not only naïve, but immoral, because you are then forced to treat people in ways that do not fit their conduct.

It is important to show why the vision of Nietzsche is mistaken, even though his appreciation of thymos is admirable, for a flourishing life. It is mistaken even from the perspective of a flourishing life. Interest and empathy with the other are needed because they contribute to one's own identity and cognitive, spiritual, and emotional development. Opposition is needed to escape from prejudice. But there must remain space for the Dionysian maverick.

---

71   2018
72   2008; 1966; 1956

A point of criticism of virtues as more or less fixed features of character is that there is little evidence of it in social psychology, where it has frequently been demonstrated that intentions are routinely disturbed by enticing or pressing impulses, and actions are determined more by circumstances than by character. However, virtues can be more or less stable inclinations that are disturbed by incidental distraction or lack of motivation, by which for a moment one is not who one wants to be, or by a misunderstanding concerning conditions, or because of multiple, conflicting loyalties one may have, as an employee, father, loved one, citizen or member of a community. Virtues develop, and refine themselves, with growing age, in experience with phronesis in varying circumstances. There is no fixed repertoire of an unchanging order of virtues.

In Aristotle's view, the good life is that of a reasonable, social and political being, oriented at the community. Virtues are part of what Kierkegaard called general ethic. A second ethic is personal conviction, with divine inspiration, which can violate morality. Levinas saw the source of this not as religion but as the face of another, who demands absolute dedication. There, relation replaces religion.

A key question is how people interact, and how they should. Is it based on self-interest or altruism, or both? An argument for self-interest is that it is in the nature of the human being to strive for its survival. Two prominent authors oriented at the other person are Emmanuel

Levinas[73] and Martin Buber[74]. They both argued that the other and the relation with him/her supersede the ego, and that other and ego may come closer to each other, but can never fuse. As Kierkegaard already argued, there remains a irreducible difference. In his play 'Huis Clos', Sartre took the dim view that 'hell, that is the other'. Indeed, the relation with the other can be conflicting, violent, but it can also be constructive, loving. The goal is to strive for the latter, and beware of the former.

Levinas and Buber made a fundamental departure from the old view, still manifested in Descartes, that the ego, the subject, has a pre-established identity, looking at the world, the object, from the outside. Hegel, and later Gadamer and Habermas, already attributed self-consciousness to interaction with another self-consciousness that recognises that of the self. Levinas and Buber, among others, objected to the Cartesian view of an autonomous self that it objectifies the other, and turns him/her into an instrument. It thereby foregoes, withers, the intrinsic, idiosyncratic value of the other. Self and other are different and cannot merge, and the other should be accepted and valued as such. This was claimed already by Vico. Hegel recognised the need for the other, saying that 'All I see in the other is his or her recognition of my identity'.[75]

For Levinas, by the epiphany of his/her 'visage', the other being 'high', 'she has to be cared for and obeyed unconditionally, in an asymmetric relationship'. Levinas'

---

73 1982, 1991, 1995
74 2004
75 Guignon and Hiley, 2003: 15

view corresponds with the tradition in CP, of militating against 'presence', the idea that things, including people, are present in the sense of 'given', fully appropriable, assimilable. The face of the other issues a call, affecting us prior to our being, and triggering the imperative to care, surrendering oneself to the other. It is not like opening the door to an existing house, but letting the other participate in building the house. This admittance of the other is unconditional. Levinas says literally that one should even accept one's henchman. In his unconditional surrender to the other, Levinas ran into the problem that the other may harm third persons, who also merit care. This requires justice, applying to all, which flies in the face of individually oriented care. This is the manifestation of a fundamental problem that also applies to Adorno's aim to recognise and implement individuality while maintaining universal justice.

You cannot make a rule that treats everyone the same and yet is tailored to unique, personal conditions. Care for the unique other must make the transition to justice for all, with rules that apply to all, and are impersonal[76]. One must somehow feel responsible not only for the unique other, but also for third parties, and ask yourself whether the one other harms other others. The asymmetry of the ideal relationship fades away, and equality under the law appears. Individualised justice would require a separate rule for everyone, and society would buckle under it.

The predicament of reconciling care dedicated to the individual other with care for other others is inevitable. That is not a good reason to withhold individual care. We

---

76 e.g. Levinas, 1991: 113–15

are often faced by this problem that doing good to one harms others. DeKey reminds us of the novel 'Night train to Lisbon', where a doctor is faced with the medical need to save a criminal with suppression and many murders to his name, while the doctor is also denounced by the community for saving this criminal. If I give money to care for victims of an earthquake, I ignore victims of other disasters.

Compare this with Kierkegaard's distinction between the 'general ethic', which is morality, and the personal ethic of conviction, which may need to transcend public morality, at the price of accepting the penalty involved. This is what the doctor in the novel does. The challenge is to balance freedom and necessity, discussed in Kierkegaard's book 'Either-Or'. According to Kierkegaard, personal ethic trumps morality.

For Buber, in contrast with Levinas, the relation had to be balanced, in dialogue. The relation, the 'between' (Buber), is prior to identity. He proposed two types of relation: The 'I-It' and the 'I-Thou' relation. In the I-It relation the other is treated as an object, instrumentally. It is 'reified', Adorno would say. In the I-Thou relationship, one is oriented at the intrinsic value of the other, letting oneself be influenced. In the terminology of Habermas, in the I-Thou relation one should engage in 'communicative action' and share a 'life world'. The I-It relation has its value, and is inevitable, but lacks depth of humanity, although it may be needed to provide the economic basis of the I-Thou relation. Inspired by Buber,

Rosa [77] pleaded for 'resonance': affecting the other and being affected by him/her, like a tuning fork sending out and picking up vibrations. I add that although it can be spontaneous, mostly resonance requires effort and dedication. One needs to immerse oneself in the other, grow understanding and empathy. One needs to immerse for resonance to emerge. If we have 'mirror neurons', that greatly helps resonance. One may have to coach the other away from closure out of fear or mistrust, try to access his/her sources of opinion and creativity, and accept such endeavours of the other on oneself.

According to Rosa, we can resonate not only with other individuals, 'horizontally', but also 'vertically', with higher level entities, such as institutions or communities, with God if one is religious, and 'diagonally', with objects. How can the latter be? According to Rosa, in resonance with things, they 'speak' to us or 'call' us. Of course, he does not mean this literally, but what, then, does it mean? The thing can also, like a person, elicit unexpected thoughts, memories, associations, emotions, feelings and actions from its hidden potential.

But how can I affect that thing? I can cherish and adorn it. I can affect its elicitation in me, by playing the piece of music or looking at the painting. I can affect the object's potential to affect me, but cannot fully control or predict what it does. An object can give ongoing surprise, and this can make it interesting and enticing. Comparably to love, friendship or trust, what the thing means to me does not wear out. Like those, it deepens in

---

77 2019

its use. Rosa [78] gives the example of a pianist who does not get bored by the piece he plays. Every time he plays, it affects him differently, but to achieve that he has to play it. In French, playing a piece is 'interpretation', which varies not only with the person playing, but also with his/her performance.

I can resonate with my writing. Formerly, before computers, writing in fluent longhand felt like playing a violin. Now, I experience hammering at a keyboard as playing a drum. Once, I whitewashed a wall and enjoyed the swish. Playing tennis, I enjoyed the 'plock' of a good hit. Can I resonate with my hammer? Formerly, craftsmen decorated their implements, and warriors their swords. Chain gangs sing. Soldiers on the march do. Perhaps craftsmen still cherish their tools, but decoration as a connection of craft with art has largely disappeared, though sometimes it appears in design.

For Bubers's I-Thou relationship and Rosa's resonance one must resist the impulse to control the other. There must be trust, but this can be violated, as I will discuss later. Rosa [79] argued that modern Man tries to control everything, which is only partly possible, and hampers the resonance that we really cherish. He argued that after the demise of the expectation of an afterlife, to fill our finite lives we want ever more than we have, which requires ever increasing efficiency, with the use of technology and the drive of capitalism, causing 'acceleration',

---

78 2020
79 2020

going faster in everything[80], and this hampers the attentive give and take of 'resonance'. This is 'bad faith': doing something we do not really want. Resonance carries uncertainty: you cannot fully control the other person, and you cannot predict every action that may arise in his or her conduct, or indeed your own. We should seek resonance of people with each other and with the natural environment. In the recent past, in the US there has been no resonance between democrats and republicans. Across the world, people avoid resonance by locking themselves into 'filter bubbles' or 'echo chambers'. Ecological disaster is looming from lack of resonance between people and nature.

Resonance is part of the *intrinsic* value of a relationship, value in itself, beyond any *extrinsic*, instrumental value. Kant already said: never value another only as an instrument, but always also as a goal.

All this rhymes with Adorno's plea for 'non-coercive identification', which can be elucidated with Bubers I-Thou relation and Rosa's resonance. Adorno pleaded to avoid what Buber called I-IT relations, which in Adorno's words are 'reifying'. According to Rosa, the absence of resonance yields *muteness*, no call or response, comparable to Buber's I-It relationship.

I-Thou relations require trust, which I add as a virtue. Trust has instrumental value, in aiding collaboration, but also has intrinsic value, as part of the quality of a relationship, in resonant I-Thou relations. As Rosa argues, excessive control is counterproductive, but on the other hand,

---

80 Rosa, 2016

if dilemmas, for example, are part of life, the urge to control them also is. From its beginnings, the human being tried to manipulate its environment, making flintstones and implements of wood and bone, and mastering fire, to give warmth and improve digestion of foods by roasting or cooking. Next to controlling impulse, reason developed for this. Such endeavour and inventiveness are part of humanity. Husbandry of animals is a form of control, but the herdsman can still resonate with his cattle.

The benefit of control depends on how far it goes. Rosa[81] identified four stages of control: making visible, making reachable, making manageable, and making useful. Excess control can mute resonance, but resonance also requires the first two stages of control, of visibility and accessibility, to achieve affect and being affected. It goes too far in the stage of making manageable, which is one-sided, and making useful, giving instrumental value, and threatening to lose intrinsic value of a relation. Rosa (2020:44) granted that resonance requires 'semi controllability.'

Part of the art of trust is moderating the urge to control, exercising the virtues of patience and resilience. One can to some extent control the conduct of others, but only partly and not always. Trust entails the acceptance of relational risk, in giving room for conduct, relinquishing control. As a result, trust is to some extent a 'leap of faith'[82]. I will further discuss trust, as needed for society, in the final chapter, on society.

The conclusion of this chapter is, that conduct is guided by virtues and vices, as personal inclinations that

---

81 2020: 17
82 Nooteboom 2002, Moellering 2009

develop along the path of life. The main virtue is phronesis, the ability to select and enact virtues according to the conditions one and one's interlocutors are in. One should strive for I-Thou relations that are reciprocal, yielding resonance, aiming at intrinsic, not only instrumental value. Those relations go beyond what is publicly established, in langue, and should delve deeper, into parole. Phronesis includes the balancing, proposed by Kierkegaard, of morals and personal conviction. The skill of phronesis develops in time, as experience in choosing virtues, their balance and enactment accrues. It learns when to deviate from langue in virtue of parole.

Existentialism and poststructuralism

To discuss existentialism, it is useful to discuss existence. Ontology is the philosophy of what exists. My favourite, up to a point, is 'Object Oriented Ontology' (OOO)[83]. A thing, or object, has an inner structure with mutually interacting elements and an outside with which it interacts. I do not agree with OOO entirely. Harman distinguishes objects from processes, to maintain the notion that an object has a lasting identity. When an airplane crashes, he sees the crash as a separate object. I disagree. I think that the object with its internal and external interactions, is processual, in a 'relational ontology'. Even a stone is a process, of moving atoms, molecular structure, heating, cooling, and erosion.

Objects are just relatively stable compared to evidently faster processes, such as things moving in time and space. This processual view does not eliminate identity, as Harman feared. Material and mental processes constitute a homeostatic system, keeping states of the system within viable boundaries, such as, in a living organism, temperature, oxygen, salinity, moisture, energy, balance of standing and walking, mental balance, red and white blood particles, immune systems, etc. In social systems also there are boundaries of actions, of what is permitted or forbidden, for the sake of the coherence and stability of the commons, and the realisation of its purpose.

---

83 Harman, 2018; Garcia, 2014

From Heidegger, Harman adopts the idea that things are not fully disclosed; you don't know all the properties even of a tool[84]. Not only do you not know in detail its atomic structure and related processes, but you also don't know all its potential. You could use a screwdriver as a hammer. Wittgenstein said 'If you want to know the meaning of a word, see how it is used'. A word is not a label on an essence, but a tool for communication, developing in its use, and its meaning can change.

Kierkegaard saw the development of the individual as going through different stages, and criticised Hegel for letting the individual evaporate in the collective entity of the state. A key question is how the realisation of existing potential can produce new potential[85]: 'potentialisation', going from the actual to the possible. Stated differently: how can objects change to the point of breaking their identity and generating a new object? (Nooteboom, 2019; 2020a). When does an organisation change its identity? When it changes its purpose, runs into inconsistencies or internal or external rivalries, usually with a change of leadership, or is taken over.

Heidegger created a revolution by no longer seeing the human being as a pre-formed subject, looking at the world from outside, but as developing in the world, in contact with other physical objects. Being is not a substantive but a verb. However, he saw the human as developing from tradition. I grant that tradition plays a role, but if you leave it at that, ignoring individual creativity,

---

84 Harman, 2002
85 Schelling, 1809

invention, innovation and art, the view becomes utterly conservative. With Heidegger, the individual diffuses, disappears, in a shared tradition. An adequate ontology must include dynamics, development, of knowledge, meaning, ethics and society, and must yield room for the individual. That forms the core of this book. The development of the individual was already proposed by Kierkegaard. Here lies the significance of existentialism.

A source of existentialism lies with Kierkegaard. I cannot claim to understand him fully, since I miss his urge for religious transcendence, he is largely incomprehensible to me, and as before with Heidegger[86], Derrida[87] and Habermas[88], I had to resort to secondary literature[89] to achieve some understanding. The problem with that is that it creates an interpretation. I read other interpretations, and sample some more, to settle on my own

For Kierkegaard, life consists of three stages. First, the 'aesthetic' stage of enjoyment of the senses, pleasure, excitement, but if that lasts too long, it derails into emptiness, boredom and insatiable, senseless consumerism. One needs to make the jump to the 'ethical' stage. Ethics is not only public morality, in shared rules of conduct, applying to everyone, but also an individual grasp of the freedom of making decisions, and taking responsibility for them. The third stage is the leap to faith and surrender to God, which deepens the personal ethic. He takes

---

86 Luckner, 1975
87 Oger, 1995
88 Dews, 1986
89 De Key, 2015

Abraham as the paradigm of deepening personal ethic to the point of violating the general ethic of protecting his son Isaac. I cannot go along with that, but I go along with the jump to ethics as individual freedom of making decisions. You don't need a God for that. Against Kierkegaard, a point of criticism is that he seems to neglect sociality in the development of the individual, so that he is in danger of falling into solipsism. That later happened also to Sartre.

Levinas rejected God but saw an absolute appeal in the visage of the other. Religion becomes relation, and relation becomes religion. We greet complete strangers, feel embarrassed in ignoring a beggar on the street. DeKey recalls the novel 'The fall' by Camus. A woman falls into the Seine, a man passes by and ignores it, and this bothers him for the rest of his life, wishing the event to be repeated, so that he can jump to the rescue.

Suppose a similar occurrence happens to you. You are walking along a canal and see someone drowning in it. You feel the urge to jump to the rescue, but you can't swim, there is a storm, and you have a small child by the hand on the slippery slope. There may be good reasons not to help, but the rest of your life it may rage in you whether you did the right thing.

Morality is contingent; it changes and depends on the situation, and thus cannot be strictly universal. Individual ethics on the other hand is unconditional, absolute, and therefore Kierkegaard assigns it to religion. There lies the task of phronesis. I accept Kierkegaard's urge for the individual not to get entangled in institutions, and to develop himself in life, and take responsibility for it.

David Hume held that benevolence towards another is innate, and I agree with that.

Freedom to take one's own path was also fearful, dizzying, to Kierkegaard, as when you are standing at the edge of a cliff, looking into it, and feel the urge to take the fearful dive into the deep. That feeling also arises when surrendering to God. For Kierkegaard, the moment where past and future meet, is the seat of freedom and faith, but we cannot know it. His paradigmatic case is marriage: one does not know what on is getting into, but makes the leap of commitment. The self cannot see itself, as an eye can see without seeing itself. The genius 'resigns everything, and then grasps everything by virtue of the absurd'. This notion of the absurd returned with Camus.[90] Camus used the example of Sisyphus, who had to labour a large stone uphill, to see it crashing down again, every time, and resigned himself to it. Like Kierkegaard, he considered the whole of life a trial, but while he remained stuck in the absurd, learning to live with it, for Kierkegaard it was a platform for faith.

Kierkegaard is the source of thinking in terms of 'difference', followed by later philosophers, for example Derrida, Levinas and Buber. As discussed: people must interact, but they will never fuse, will always remain separate. Kierkegaard opposed Hegel, for surrendering difference, in an ultimate synthesis.

Later came Nietzsche, with his predilection for Dionysus and thymos, the urge to manifest oneself, in a 'philosophy of life'. The self is mangled by institutions. Oskar Negt and Alexander Kluge claimed in their book 'History

---

90 Kierkegaard, 1941: 51

and obstinacy' ('Geschichte und Eigensinn'), that because of the obstinacy or idiosyncrasy and 'self-regulation' of work, difference or otherness is never tamed'.

Sartre claimed that 'Existence precedes essence'. The human being develops his/her identity in action, is in essence free, and cannot shove responsibility off onto conditions, even in extreme situations. You are always free to say no (or think it). I agree with Sartre that the self is not pre-established, but has an innate potential of development, and develops its identity in interaction with the world. However, that does not mean that he is free.

Wittgenstein claimed that systems of rules are like games, such as chess or soccer. If you don't play by the rules, you are excluded. The suggestion is that you can switch to another game, but you have to abide by its rules again, or you have to invent a new one, and how can you get that accepted and widely played? He said that 'if you want to know the meaning of a word, see how it is used'. That can change.

Structuralism in Hermeneutics had scientific aspirations. A text is autonomous, determined by grammar, not psychology, not dependent on context or reader, as earlier Hermeneutics claimed. I generalise that, in the claim that structures are regulative, and do not depend on interpretations or context. Structuralists elaborate the order of regulative structures that an individual is entangled in. It leaves little liberty. Poststructuralism however, seeks room for deviation. To call myself a post-structuralist does not mean that I am against structure. Structure is inevitable, but I am seeking a structure which is not too bureaucratic, is porous, with fissures through which individuals can creep and have some freedom.

Nietzsche deplored the strictures that society and morality imposed. So did Adorno. Adorno went so far as to say 'All participation, all humanitarianism of contact and participation is only a mask of a tacit acceptance of the inhuman.'[91] But to avoid it, on must avoid society.

A follower of Nietzsche, Michel Foucault,[92] objected to old views of the 'presence' of signs and meanings, as entities observed in the same way by all and always. Meanings vary with perspective. He explored cases where a dominant language game dominated marginal and dissident people, as in organisations of care, such as medical clinics, prisons, homes for the insane, and scientific communities, where inmates or participants are subjected to ideologies and regimes that are mostly tacit, taken for granted, and accepted by the inmates even if they are victims of it. I propose that this applies more widely, in organisations, such as firms, schools, universities, ministries, municipalities and professional societies. If you do not conform, you are cast out or disciplined. In his early work, Foucault focussed on negative power and the suppression it yields. In his later work he recognised that power can also be positive.

One of the studies of Foucault was of the development, genealogy, of the penal system. It used to employ torture, but now that is scarce, but there still is punishment. In the 'panopticum' of Bentham (a circular structure with the guards in the middle), the guards can see

---

91 Adorno, 2003: 27
92 1994, 2002Ki

the prisoners in all directions, and the prisoners feel observed even when they are not.

A point of criticism of Foucault, which may apply also to the present book, is that he fights structuralism in a structuralist way, in setting out a general process of the emergence of suppressive systems.

A recent development is that of 'restorative justice'[93], in which the aim is less to protect society by locking up criminals, and more on helping criminals to re-integrate in society, by confronting criminal and victim, coaching the criminal to see the harm he has done and to 'better' his life, and getting the victim to understand the criminal's circumstances, and perhaps even forgive him. Perhaps Foucault would see this as merely part of manipulation.

A second study by Foucault was that of sexuality. That also includes forces of surveillance, categorisation, normalisation and training. A recent development here is that of 'LHBTI'), which tries to escape from established sexual categorisation.

Foucault sees power everywhere. I take the customary definition of power as the ability to affect the choices of others. This can be negative, in restraining the room of choice or imposing a choice, but can also extend the room for choice, eliminating obstacles or giving access to resources, enabling people. They often go together, for example in the position in a network. The question is which dominates. In his early studies, Foucault focussed on negative power and the suppression it yields. Later he also acknowledged that power can be positive.

---

93 Claesen, 2022

Elimination of the negative side of power is an illusion. Society is a system, like an organism. Its elements yield the whole, with its benefits, but to do so, the elements have to accept restrictions. In society, people and institutions are its elements. Berlin[94] distinguished between 'negative' and 'positive' freedom. Negative freedom is absence or paucity of outside constraints on individual action, of laws, morality, and customs. Positive freedom is access to the means of existence and flourishing, such as housing, food, movement, communication, and protection, for example. To achieve the benefits of society, one must accept the limitation of negative freedom. This is reminiscent of Adorno's claim that society inevitably limits the scope for the flourishing of people, in more or less suppression or indoctrination.

According to Horkheimer and Adorno, in current society people become de-individualised by roles that are imposed by capitalism. I am not sure this is particular to capitalism. Did that not also occur under communism? It occurs in any society, because that is a system.

The deeper problem that Horkheimer and Adorno identified in their 'Dialectic of the Enlightenment', following Weber, was that while the Enlightenment strove to abolish myth, itself developed the myth of reason, where, in Weber's words, 'instrumental rationality' crowds out 'goal rationality' of human existence. What now with criticism, if it is sidetracked by instrumental rationality? According to Adorno, the answer lies in art, since that is non-instrumental. This prescinds Foucault's escape from institutional oppression by 'building your life as a work of art'.

---

94 1969

Adorno rejected philosophical systems[95], on the ground that they freeze the flow of thought. That position is untenable, because if that is so, why write a book, as Adorno did? On the contrary, philosophical thought is legitimate if it becomes coherent in a system, with elements supporting each other, like a house of cards. I grant that as a book progresses, it shifts ideas, and is never finished, but in doing so it can contribute to, or exhibits, the development of thoughts. In their coherence, ideas have some stability, because the system as a whole cannot shift instantly. Elsewhere, Adorno pleaded for such interdisciplinary coherence. Books are never finished. In this way, there seems to be limited opportunity for autonomy. This bothered Foucault in his later work, and he could not do better than plead for 'living your life as a work of art'. How is that to be done? One is rooted more or less deeply in multiple networks that are more or less constrictive. One can 'play them off' against each other, compensating constriction here with relative freedom elsewhere. People do that in many ways, in compensating strict regimes in work with more lax sports clubs, families or friendships. Furthermore, as discussed in the chapter on language, language has the private, idiosyncratic dimension of parole, which yields some scope to hide from the order of langue.

In sum, my position is 'poststructuralist', saying that yes, there are restrictions, but there are holes one can creep through.

Most people enter multiple networks, to obtain economic, social, intellectual and symbolic capital

---

95 O'Connor, 2013: 21

(Bourdieu). Symbolic capital is prestige, beauty, renown, media exposure, resources for exhibitory conduct, flouting possessions. Items in a network are more or less connected. Perhaps one thinks of Deleuze's notion of 'rhyzome', where any item can connect with any other, and there is no hierarchy. Most networks do have some hierarchy. There is a large literature on networks, dealing with structure, boundaries, nesting in larger systems, the tension between autonomy of its members and their conformance to shared rules, collaboration, rivalry, differences of their position in the structure, and 'structural holes' between them, i.e. lack of connections. Like any organisation, a network also requires adherence to some sort of 'focus', with modes of communication and procedures, but it is often less strict than in other organisations. Network analysis clarifies the notion of 'polycentrality', attributed to 'commons': people in it have more or less autonomy, are different, in private goals and means, and everyone has to balance individual autonomy and conformance to shared rules. There are, however, differences in power, depending on position and role, but, as noted before, power can be positive.

There are technical, physical networks, of utilities, (gas, water, electricity, communication), and distribution of goods . Here I focus on the social networks of commons, of which there is a multitude: communities, firms, associations (of professions, trades, research, entrepreneurs), unions, teams, guilds, cooperatives, interest groups, and lobby groups. If one is in multiple networks, one is an attractive partner, which yields an accumulation of contacts. The rich get richer, in a 'Matthew effect'.

Lower educated people with less prestigious jobs are in few networks, and tend to be excluded from them, yielding great inequality in society. This may be a new class theory, to replace that of Marxism. Exclusion is often not direct, targeted, but the result of lacking the prior capital needed to contribute to the network. Low educated lack intellectual capital. Intellectuals often lack social and symbolic capital. Knowledge and understanding beyond science used to belong to the elite, but no longer.

Figure 4 connected networks

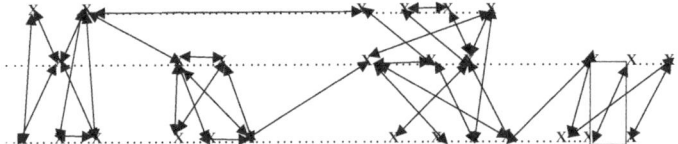

Not to become closed clubs, social networks can be mutually connected, but more sparsely than within the network. There are 'boundary spanners', which have connections with at least one node in another network, next to internal ties. Concerning governance, the position of a boundary spanner can be precarious, needing to conform to the internal order, to some extent, but also to the order in the outside network, if it connects to one, and that may jeopardise its internal legitimacy.

Knowledge networks are a special case. They all use or produce knowledge of some form, but knowledge commons have specific properties and problems of governance. Frischmann et al.[96] give the following examples of knowledge commons with different forms of the governance of

---

96 2014

production, property, access, and exclusion: Associations of aircraft producers, open source software production (such as Linux), Wikipedia, press associations, fan communities. Often, networks are not designed, and emerge spontaneously.

This tendency to create networks is ancient, and grew in evolution, becoming instinctive. Even at the time that humans were still hunter-gatherers, they needed to collaborate in groups, for hunting large prey, protection, or to wage war. There were occasional links between the groups, for trade and exchange of brides, preventing incest.[97]

Networks can be sparse, with each node having one relation with another node, but few more. Or it can be dense, with many nodes having relations with more other nodes. With n nodes, the maximum density, with every node being connected with all the other nodes, is $n(n-1)/2$. There is a diseconomy of scale here. If everyone communicates with everyone else, this is likely to jeopardise productive activity.

There are different types of position within networks. One key position in a network is that of high 'degree centrality', with many direct links to others. This feeds upon itself, attracting ever more direct links. It may develop into a 'hub', through which indirect links to others flow. Large airports are often hubs, for flights to collect passengers from different directions. A central position yields power of access to many resources. A drawback may be that one is so entangled in many relations as to have little room for manoeuvre, and may get locked up in them. Recently, the Dutch airport Schiphol abolished night

---

97 Moseley, 2019; Tomassello, 2016

flights, to reduce the noise nuisance for people living nearby, but was indicted by the airlines, and was ordered to withdraw the decision.

Another characteristic position is that of 'network centrality', a crossroads of paths from other nodes to each other. Here one can get information from many sources, but this may exceed its absorptive capacity.

Another position is that on the periphery, with limited contacts inside the network and also connections with other networks. This can yield new information, as a source of renewal, but may raise suspicions from within the home network. Having contacts with outsiders may be seen as dubious, eliciting betrayal.

Relations require investments. A special kind of investments discussed in 'Transaction Cost Economics' is 'specific investments'. Those have value in a relation but not outside it, due to dedicated instruments or facilities, training staff, and the building of trust. This creates vulnerability, in making parties dependent. The least dependent party can threaten to break the relation unless he gets a larger share of jointly produced value. A remedy for this is to share ownership of the asset. An alternative is to offer such exceptional value in the relation that the other side would not want to exit.

Ties can be 'rich', with many resources involved, large 'specific investments', in the sense indicated before, yielding mutual dependence, or 'thin', yielding little dependence. Networks do not necessarily entail friendship, but they do require trust. According to 'Dunbar's number' of around 150, one can hardly have more friends than that, while networks can include many more people.

The conclusion of this chapter is that life is engagement and choice, acting in networks, acquiring and supplying capital, wielding and being subjected to positive and negative power, and judiciously exercising trust. According to some philosophers, relation replaces religion. Dedication to one other, however, can become at odds with justice for all, as discussed before.

Society

In CP, society is the most hated structure. But the development of personal identity arises from interaction with culture, and culture arises from interaction between people. They need each other. Identity loses its connotation of 'sameness'. Someone's identity maintains its difference with respect to others, and is different from that of his past. It develops from inherited potential, along a personal path of life. Part of a person's identity is hidden, as Freud taught us. The identity of a nation is wrapped in its ideology and culture. The development of culture is mediated by interaction between people, in the acquisition of what Bourdieu called economic, social, intellectual and symbolic capital. Symbolic capital is prestige, renown, possessions (showing off), appearance (e.g. on TV, in shows, on social media), publications, etc.

Does Aristotelian multiple causality also apply to the development of society and culture? I think it does. Society develops by the change of goals of people, the development of their means, methods, conditions, and examples they pursue. Early society had to cope with limited means, methods, knowledge, and from early times sought higher powers to explain the incomprehensible, and yielded models of conduct to follow. How this interaction works out is difficult to predict, and while there are these causes, there is no fixed development of societies apart from the regularity of their emergence, blossoming, and decline. The causes are enhanced or constrained by laws of mathematics or physics, as part of the conditional cause. Climate can change as part of that cause, or it can be manmade, as in the exploration of materials, inventions, and wars.

Culture has four meanings. One is that it is manmade, in contrast with nature. It mostly destroys nature, but it can also mean cultivating it, such as in the 'culture' of grapes. A third meaning is anthropological: habits, customs, rituals, institutions, rules, norms, ethics, by which people live and interact. A fourth meaning is heritage, in the form of art, architecture, infrastructure, also called 'civilisation'.

Institutions are manmade rules and conditions for action, such as laws and language. They are 'enabling constraints'. A road through a swamp is constraining, in that one must keep to it not to fall into the swamp, but it does get you across the swamp. People can contribute to the development of institutions, often in a joint effort in a network, such as private and public organisations, political parties, associations, clubs, conspiracies, etc. Individuals affect culture, by their actions, e.g. by creating art, but that is affected by styles and schools of art. They can write books, but their acceptance depends on fashion, renown of the author, entertainment value and connection with the news. Networks develop their own subculture, with shared goals, procedures, habits, morality and governance.

Language enables us to communicate, imposing established meanings, grammar, syntax, locutions, sayings. Can one make language? Not by oneself.

Sometimes idiosyncratic language, parole, can catch on and become shared, public, in some community.

Culture varies between countries, as a result of their histories, but can also overlap, more or less, depending also on their geography, trade, or supra-national arrangements, such as the EU. An example of the effect of history is how long people remained nomadic before settling down in agriculture and husbandry. Nomads can flee from the reputation effects of conduct, but when settled in agriculture, they could not flee from them. An example of geography is the effect of climate, the presence of waterways for transport, access to the sea with harbours, depending on the rockiness of the coast. Because of that, Ireland had no shipping and fishing, and was restricted to agriculture, and vulnerable to famine from crop disease. Some overlaps of culture occur in fairly universal moral injunctions, such as the condemnation of murder and incest and the protection of property. All this is perhaps too obvious to mention.

We cannot do without markets, as the failure of communism demonstrates. Friedrich von Hayek[98] argued that only the decentralised forces of demand and supply can cater to the local diversity of the needs and desires of people, and local initiatives. Competition is a 'discovery device', Hayek said. It makes the economy exciting, adventurous, and risky. But Hayek neglected the imperfections of markets. Those are various. Concentration in large firms can yield manipulation of markets, by blocking entry of competitors, threatening ruinous price

---

98 1945

competition until the newcomer is scared off, lobbying in government to obtain special subsidies, tax advantages, and lax rules concerning the environment, under the motto of a favourable 'investment climate', with employment as hostage, in blackmail, threatening to withdraw it if it does not get its way.

The system properties of society yield a challenge to democracy, especially because to achieve its potential, the interaction of its elements, the people, it requires the commitment to accept the limitation of negative freedom for the sake of positive freedom, and to deliberate with people one expects to disagree with, which people are increasingly unwilling or unable to do. Democracy requires a measure of altruism and commitment to common causes and it is corroding in the lack of it.

A tragedy of democracy is that out of a democratic drive to satisfy citizens, and to avoid loss of votes to populist parties, who bank on complaints of citizens, the government accumulates laws and regulations that clog up and expand the bureaucratic system until it becomes inoperable.

Democratic governments are pressed by their constituents to offer additional benefits, in grants, subsidies or relief, but this labours under the dilemma of benevolence and equal justice, leading to a ratchet effect of benevolence concerning the special needs of some group, which in turn evokes claims of injustice, and demands for equal treatment from all others. Also, when dedicated to specific groups, every new regulation requires control against misuse, necessitating formal bureaucratic procedures that are felt to be inhumane, which evokes further measures, complicating the procedure and intensifying the perception of bureaucratic, inhumane meddling. It is difficult to abolish benefits, which come to be seen as inalienable rights. The more regulation is added, the greater the chance that it becomes in conflict with already existing regulations. The system of regulations and control gets clogged up. I call it ' institutional crowding'. I am not the first to say this. Habermas already said that 'it seems that system imperatives are encroaching on areas which are demonstrably unable to perform their roles if they are removed from communicatively structured domains of action.'[99]

This can evoke protests against the encroachment of bureaucracy in private affairs, what Habermas called the 'life world', in a conservative plea for a return to simple, traditional, semi religious, authoritarian, racist, anti-feminist and nationalistic values. I think this is what is happening now. This seems to ignore the underlying aim of government to provide care and support, but this is engulfed by conspiracy theories concerning a vicious 'elite' that suppresses and exploits the population.

Democracy demands a certain measure of altruism, to limit self-interest for consideration of others and contributions to the common cause, as in paying taxes. But when and to what extent are people altruistic? De Dreu et al[100] proposed the notion of 'parochial altruism'. People are altruistic (to some extent) towards people in the group they feel they belong to, but are suspicious with regard to outsiders. This, I propose, also derives from evolution and thus is instinctive.

---
99 Habermas, 1986
100 2014

This is because altruism in the group contributes to its survival. True, properties are transmitted in the first place by genes, which are individual. If benevolence prevails, the group becomes vulnerable to the invasion of opportunists, who survive in preying on indigenous altruism. Thus for survival of the group, a sufficient number of people should be able to identify and block the outsiders. Hence an instinct of suspicion of outsiders evolved. This causes xenophobia. Outsiders are most readily identified on the basis of their skin colour, dress, cooking and demeanour. Hence racism and discrimination are instinctive and so difficult to eradicate. A way to remedy that is to broaden the horizon of the group one feels to belong to. That is done, for example, in collaboration with the refugees in jobs or social groups, to discover that they are similar to us.

De Dreu et al. administered oxytocin, the 'love hormone', to people, and expected suspicion towards outsiders to decrease, but found the opposite. Altruism increased towards insiders, but decreased further towards outsiders. Parochial altruism deepened.

The systemic nature of society implies that complete autonomy of people, the desire for which was whipped up by the Enlightenment, is impossible.

Since some continental philosophers give sweeping statements against markets, as part of capitalism and associated AP., I will go deeper into the issue, and will give a brief lesson in economics.

In some cases, markets are counterproductive or do not work, as in prizes and diploma's. A Nobel prize would

not work if it could be bought, and bought diploma's would ruin the value of education. Sandel[101] gave the example of a concert in the park in New York, that the mayor wanted to offer the citizens for free. Due to a limited capacity, however, people had to collect a ticket, but this caused long queues, and a clever entrepreneur had vagrants wait in line for a pittance, and he sold the resulting tickets to the highest bidder, so that in the end mostly rich people attended the concert, against the intention. When markets are desirable, they have imperfections that need redress. These differ for different industries, but policymakers mostly don't know them. Appropriate policies depend on the following features:
- The perspicacity of the quality of the good or service offered
- Economy of scale in production or marketing, producing concentration, which limits competition
- Transaction costs
- Separability of producing or marketing goods

Concerning perspicacity of quality, there is a distinction between 'search goods', whose quality one can judge before purchase, such as cars and washing machines, 'experience goods', whose quality one can judge during consumption, such as concerts, restaurants and holidays, and 'credence goods', whose quality one cannot judge even after consumption, such as a consultant or garage. This raises a demand for reporting services, such as the review of a concert or restaurant, or a brand name or association that guarantees the quality of its members, which it promises to guard.

---

101 2012

There are several economies of scale, such as costs of the capacity of a process of production and marketing. Here, the capacity of production, and hence the proceeds, of a chemical reactor depends on the third power of the radius of the reactor, while the costs depend on its surface, in radiation of heat, cleaning, weight and transport. Productivity then depends on the ratio between surface and content, which decreases with the radius.

That is why at the North Pole animals are large and bulbous, such as whales, walruses and polar bears. How, then, one may ask, are there also large bulbous animals around the equator, such as elephants, hippopotamuses and buffalos? The issue is not coldness of the environment that needs to be kept out, but also a matter of keeping out the heat in a hot climate. Why, then, are there also elongated, slender animals such as cheetahs, in the tropics? In the explosion of speed in the pursuit of a prey, they generate heat themselves, which they need to radiate out. When not in pursuit, they lie panting in the shadow of trees.

A second economy of scale arises from the indivisibility of resources, such as an attendant at a cash register or point of call. When business is slow, the attendant is idle most of the time. Formerly, small shops could survive because a shopkeeper could do home chores until the store bell tingled and the shopkeeper rushed downstairs to serve. This temporary idle capacity also applies e.g. to truck drivers, stuck in traffic. In a Jumbo jet several effects occur simultaneously: the bulbous shape of the plane to save fuel, and the occupation of the pilot.

Transaction costs are costs associated with the market, such as search costs for supply and demand, costs of contract, costs of monitoring and control, and litigation in the case of conflict. These costs are the higher the higher relational risk and size of the investment involved. A special case here is so-called 'specific investments' that have worth only in a specific relation, which invites opportunism: If A has made the investment, partner B is tempted to demand a greater share in jointly produced profit, or else he will exit and leave A with a worthless investment. Such one-sided risk can be reduced or eliminated, by sharing the ownership of the asset. It may however be that precisely that investment will make A supply a unique contribution that makes him a monopolist.

The inseparability of assets of production or distribution, such as hardware and software stimulates the producer to offer only proprietary software, and thereby become a monopolist.

According to Adorno, to achieve some degree of autonomy under the sway of society, one needs 'Bildung', intellectual and spiritual development in harmony with nature, with moral awareness and regard to others. He admits that is something of the past, as something only an elite could achieve, and furthermore it is not enough.

Elites are inevitable. Raymond Aron said it well[102]: 'The problem requiring research is not the existence of a minority holding wealth and power, but the nature of the minority's composition, the means it uses to maintain itself in power, the number of intermediary groups, and

---

102 2017: 62

the opportunities given to the greater number of people'. Lenin deliberately strove for centralised, absolute power of the communist party. Trotsky warned that this power would first go to the party, then the central committee, and then to its general secretary, which it did. In an army, there is a chain of command. In democracies, elites arise, of politicians in government and parliament, top-ranking civil servants, CEO's of banks and large companies, a central bank, leaders of a variety of institutions, such as NGO's, health organisations, and so on. The elite tends to be well-educated, well positioned in networks, and often more focussed on their careers than on the common good. They are usually strong in rhetoric, obfuscation, procrestination, mutual squabbles, and are tied down in compromises. But street gangs also grow leaders, as well as soccer clubs, investment clubs, congregations, protest groups, and so on. A populist party militates against elites, but if it wins an election, the first thing it will do is institute an elite of its own.

Communication between people is needed for society, in deliberation, parliament, management, media, gossip, education, and meetings. It requires trust in people and institutions.

Trust is a complicated notion.[103] It requires trustworthiness. How does one determine and influence that? Trust is emotional, because it is related to risk, but it can also be rational, in analysing the sources of trustworthiness. There is trust in competence, the ability to honour expectations, and intentional trust, the intention to do so to the best of one's ability. If people lose trust in politics and

---

103 Nooteboom, 2002

government, national or local, is this loss of belief in their competence, ability to get things done, or loss of trust in intention to realise their promises?

Competence is often judged by speed and efficiency, while effectiveness and the goal of policies are more important. There can be trust and distrust on several levels: Persons, organisations, and the wider institutional environment. During the banking crisis, did we lose trust in bankers, banks, financial markets or government intervention? People are now said to still trust the democratic system, but not individual politicians.

Table 1: sources of intentional trust

	outside the relationship	inside the relationship
control	contracts, reputation	hierarchy, incentives
trust	morality, culture	family, clan, friendship

To have trust, one usually needs to have it on all levels. In table 1, I give a survey of the sources of intentional trust. Along the top row are effects of control, appealing to self-interest. This can be based on forces outside the relation, such as laws and reputation, and measures inside relationships, such as hierarchy and incentives. Along the bottom row are factors beyond control, in public morality, in the left column of factors outside the relation, and on the right solidarity between clan- or family members.

An advantage of trust is that it enables the reciprocity of the I-Thou relations proposed by Buber, the intrinsic value of relations in the communicative action proposed by Habermas, discussed before. An economic disadvantage of clan-based trust is that it locks people up inside the clan, robbing relations from the challenges and opportunities of outside competition. The table illustrates the dilemma of capitalist society, between high quality, humanistic relations and the reifying relations of control, for the sake of competition and efficiency.

What drives societal change? Perhaps, here also we can use the six-fold causality of Aristotle:

Efficient cause: racism and exclusion of immigrants, formation and derailment of elites, in less attention to citizens with little education.

Final cause: democracy, keeping national identity and culture pure, the seeking of enjoyment and excitement, morality.

Material cause: the national economy, food prices, inflation, scarcity of resources.

Formal cause: education, research, the arts, morality.

Conditional cause: globalisation, war, as in Ukraine, climate.

Exemplary cause: Trump as an example for extreme right, as with Bolsonaro in Brasil, idols, influencers, inebriation of false news and conspiracy plots.

As in knowledge, language, identity and ethics, discussed in the previous chapters, dynamics is key in society, and satisfies most of the complaints against earlier philosophy by CP.

A conclusion of this chapter, against most CF, is that a social system, in order to achieve its benefits, must limit the autonomy of its elements, people and institutions, maintaining a homeostasis. Both positive and negative power are inevitable, and are suppressive but also beneficial. The structure of society is broken up by wars, environmental calamities, and revolution, art and entrepreneurship.

A second conclusion, consistent with this, is that one can strive for non-reifying, humanistic I-Thou relations that are conducive to the development of identity and 'the good life'.

A third conclusion is that this requires the art of trust, which can be both emotional and rational.

Summary and conclusions

The whole of CP is difficult to summarise. There is a German thread of Kant, Hegel, and Marx, clinging to the Enlightenment ideal of rationality and systemic structure, but Vico, Schelling, Hamann, Adorno, Heidegger and Habermas deviate, in militating against oppressive structures of social, political, and scientific systems, though Habermas maintains an ideal of rational discourse. He militates against the obsession with difference in poststructuralism, and argues for crossing this distance, dealing with both similarity and commonality, in discourse. He upheld his view of 'communicative action', though that was already in Hegel. Social interaction is relatively neglected in later poststructuralism.

The development of CP radicalises in the later thread of French philosophies preluded by Nietzsche and Heidegger, of: Lyotard, Foucault, Derrida, and Rorty, though the latter is not French, and Sartre, with the nihilistic extreme of Baudrillard. But where do we fit Hume, who preluded much of the French scepticism?

A 'fingerprint', summary of characteristics, of the French thread of CP is as follows:

1. Rejection of 'totalising', 'logocentric', universalist theories with a stable, fixed foundation. Theories are just 'language games'. No 'grand narratives', just 'little' ones.

2. No 'presence', fixed identity, of anything. People, words, meanings are subject to flux and change.
3. Respect and defence of irreducible difference between people, words, and meanings.
4. No static conceptual or social structure, which is seen as inevitably authoritarian and suppressive.
5. Interdisciplinarity.
6. Pragmatism.

I agree with most of these points, but concerning number 1, I maintain science and theory, but grant that those are limited, temporary, partial, and depend on background knowledge that cannot fully become explicit, and depends on perspective and context. I disagree with number 4. Structures are inevitable, with more or less authority, which is not necessarily suppressive. In its radicalism, this line of CP threatens to lose its pragmatism. No theory means no policy analysis, no ethics blocks social coherence. In spite of the rhetoric against structure, Foucault structured the emergence of suppressive institutions. He averred that he did not use causality[104], but this is empty gesturing: talking about how institutions create suppression is talking causality.

Habermas militated against point 2. To maintain difference is to block communication. But I propose that there can be similarity without identity, with communication building on what is similar and profiting from what is different, with what I call 'cognitive distance', and 'crossing' it. Without difference, communication would lose its dynamics, innovativeness.

---

104 Sims, 2000: 51

Old philosophy, in particular AP, ostracised metaphysics for not being amenable to verification. With the points in the above fingerprint, the later French continental philosophers unabashedly revived metaphysics, denying the possibility of verification[105].

A thread running through all chapters of this book is dynamics. Knowledge, meaning, morality and society are not so much states as processes of development. The 'cycle of discovery' is a model of the development of knowledge from experience. It rhymes with the 'hermeneutic circle, a model of the interaction of the general and the particular, which generates new meanings. As Wilhelm von Humboldt said, language is product and process.[106] In life, living requires development and realisation of an identity, in a plunge into uncertainty. In ethics, the notion of 'phronesis' indicates how virtues and their enactment develop. Societies develop from the interaction of culture and individuals. Much of this development can be understood by the six-fold causality of Aristotle.

Related to dynamics, CP opposes the notion of 'presence', as if things are static and knowable. Fundamentals are static, so that this opposition to 'presence' is related to the opposition of CP to fundamentalism.

Another thread of CP is a focus on individuals rather than universals. Part of their rejection of science is that it pretends to be universal, 'totalising', and thereby suppressive. In ethics, phronesis may be compared to Lyotard's 'little narratives', coping with everyday vicissitudes,

---

105 Sims, 2000: 202
106 Sherrat 2006: 62

without a universal, context-independent universal moral order. There are generalities that abstract from individuals, and shift as they are applied to individuals that act in a diversity of contexts, in the hermeneutic circle. That applies to knowledge, also in science, meanings in language, morality and the enactment of virtues, and culture in societies.

A third thread is how these ideas reflect the earlier ideas of Adorno, such as those on 'understanding, reification, mediation, dialectics, interaction of subject and object, and identification', and the later ideas of post-structuralist French philosophers, indicated in the above 'fingerprint'.

A fourth thread is that a society is a system, which yields what its separate parts cannot, but to achieve this inevitably imposes constraints on its elements. A society that imposes no constraints on people, as Horkheimer and Adorno seem to want, is impossible. Constraints imposed by an elite are inevitable. One can only seek a system with constraints that are as humanistic as possible. Democracy seeks such a society, but often fails, and then becomes authoritarian.

A concept that appears in all chapters, in different ways, is that of 'homeostasis'. In any system, constraints are imposed on the elements and their relations in the system, for the system to achieve coherence in its functioning and goals. In science, one finds this in the injunction not to affect the 'hard core' of a 'research programme'. In language, established public meanings of concepts, in 'langue', on the 'paradigmatic axis' of the 'hermeneutic circle', constrain the variety of individual 'parole', on the 'syntagmatic axis'. In society, individual action and institutions are constrained by culture, with its ideology and morality. These limitations of 'negative freedom' are not all inescapable. Genius escapes from the hard core of science, poetry from langue, artists and rebels from culture.

The six-fold causality of Aristotle appears in all chapters, driving action, interaction, change of meaning, virtues, and society.

References

Adorno, T.W. 2003, *Minima Moralia*, Frankfurt: Suhrkamp.

Angle and M. Slote (eds.) 2003, *Virtue ethics and Confucianism*: 162-70, New York: Routledge.

Aron, R.2017, *In defense of decadent Europe,* New York: Routledge.

Austin, J.L. 1955, *How to do things with words*, William James Lecture, Harvard.

Berlin I. 1969, *Two concepts of liberty,* Edinburgh: Edinburgh University Press.

.... 1976, *Three critics of the Enlightenment,* Princeton University Press.

Bernstein, R.J. 2003, 'Rorty's inspirational liberalism', in: Guignon, C. and D. Hiley (eds.), *Richard Rorty*, Cambridge University Press.

Best, S and D. Kellner 2003, *Postmodernism,* in: R.G. Solomon and David Sherman (eds.), *Continental Philosophy*, Blackwell.

Boden, M.A. 1979, *Piaget*, Fontana.

Bowie, A. 1993, *Schelling and modern European philosophy*, London: Routledge.

Buber, M 2004), *Ich und Du,* Gütersloh, Güttersloher Verlaghaus.

Claessen, J. & A. van Hoek 2022, *Herstelrecht door de ogen van,* Boom.

Critchley, S, 2001, *Continental Philosophy: a very short introduction,* Oxford University Press.

Cullen, B 1994, 'Philosophy of existence 3: Merleau-Ponty', Kearny, R. (ed.), 1994, *ontinental philosophy in the 20th century*, Milton Park: Routledge: 105-30.

Damasio, A 2003, *Looking for Spinoza; Joy, sorrow and the feeling brain*, Orlando FA: Harcourt.

Dews, P.1986, *Habermas*, interviews, London: Verso.

Desmond, W. 1994, Philosophies of religion: Marcel, Jaspers, Levinas, in: Kearny, R, (ed *Continental philosophy in the 20th century*, Milton Park: Routledge: 131-75.

Edelman, G.M. 1987, *Neural Darwinism: The theory of neuronal group selection*, New York: Basic Books.

Flavell, J.H.1967, *The developmental psychology of Jean Piaget*, Princeton, NJ: Van Nostrand.

Foucault, M. 1994, '*Dits et Ecrits*, Gallimard.

Frege, G. 1892, *On sense and reference*, (In German), Zeitschrift fur Philosophie und philosophische Kritik, 100: 25-50.

Frischman B.M., M. Madison, & K J S. Strandberg (eds,), 2014, *Governing knowledge commons, Oxford University Press.*

Garcia, T. 2015 *Form and Object: A Treatise on Things*, trans. M.A. Ohm & J. Cogburn. Edinburgh: Edinburgh University Press.

Greenfield, S. 2000, *The private life of the brain*, Penguin.

Guignon, C. and D. Hiley. 2003, *Richard Rorty*, Cambridge University Press.

Habermas, J. 1982, *Theory of Communicative action'(Theorie des Kommunikativen Handelns,* Frankfurt: Suhrkamp.

.... 1984, *preliminary studies and elaborations of the theory of communicative action (Vorstudien and Ergänzungen zur Theorie des kommunikativen Handelns)*, Frankfurt: Suhrkamp.

Hall, E.T. 1967, *Beyond culture*. Anchor.

Harman, G. 2018. *Object-Oriented Ontology: A New Theory of Everything*. London: Pelican.

.... 2002, *Tool-Being: Heidegger and the Metaphysics of Objects*. Chicago: Open Court.

Hayek, Friedrich von. 1945, 'The use of knowledge in society', *American Economic Review*, 35/ 4, 519– 30.

Heidegger, M. 1993, *Sein und Zeit,* Tübingen: Max Niemeyer Verlag.

Horkheimer M and T Adorno 1986, *Dialektik der Aufklärung*, Frankfurt am Main: Fisher Taschenbuch Verlag.

De Key, J. 2015, *Kierkegaard anders gezien*, Zoetermeer: Klement.

Kearny, R, 1994, *Continental philosophy in the 20th century*, Milton Park: Routledge.

Lakatos, I. 1978 *The methodology of scientific research programmes* Cambridge: Cambridge University Press.

.... and Alan Musgrave 1970, *Criticism and the growth of knowledge,* Cambridge: Cambridge University Press.

Lakoff, G. and M. Johnson. 1980, *Metaphors we live by*, Chicago, IL: University of Chicago Press.

Levinas, E. 1995, *Alterité et transcendance,* Paris: Fata Morgana.

.... 1982, *De l'évasion,* Paris: Fata Morgana.

.... 1991, *Entre nous, Essays sur le penser-à-láutre*, Paris: Grasset.

Malakowski A. 2013, *Cambridge companion to Pragmatism*, Cambridge: Cambridge University Press.

Madison, G.B. 1994, 'Hermeneutics: Gadamer and Ricouer', in: Kearny, R. (ed.) *Continental philosophy in the 20th century,* Milton Park: Routledge.

Merleau-Ponty, M. 1964, *Le visible et l'invisible,* Gallimard

.... 1963, *The structure of behavior*, Beacon Press.

Moseley, Roger. 2019, *Morality: A natural history*, Victoria, BC: Friesen Press.

Negt, O. and A. Kluge 2014, *History and obstinacy*. Zone Books.

Nietzsche, F.2008, *Morgenröte,* Munich: Deutsche Taschenbuch Verlag, de Gruyter.

.... 1966, *Beyond good and evil*, New York: Vintage.

.... 1956, *The birth of tragedy and the genealogy of morals*, New York: Doubleday.

Nooteboom, B. 2000, *Learning and innovation in organisations and economies*, Oxford: Oxford University Press.

.... 2002, *Trust, Forms, foundations, functions, failures and figures* Cheltenham UK: Edward Elgar.

O'Connor, B. 2013, *Adorno*, London: Routledge.

Oger, E 1995, *Jacques Derrida*, Kapellen: Pelckmans.

Piaget, J.1974, *Introduction ⊠ lépistemologie genetique,* Paris: Presses Universitaires de France.

Ramos, S. 2014, *Profile of Man and culture,* Google.

Sandel, M 2012, *What money can't buy*, Allen Lane/Penguin.

Saussure, F de 1979, *Cours de Linguistique Générale*, Paris: Payotèque, Payot.

Searle, J.R. 1969 *Speech Acts: An essay in the philosophy of language,* Cambridge: Cambridge University Press.

Schelling, F.W.J. *Philosophical Enquiries Into the Nature of Human Freedom and Matters Connected Therewith*, trans. J. Gutman. Chicago: Open Court, 1936 [1809].

Sherrat, Y. 2006, *Continental philosophy of social science,* Cambridge: Cambridge University Press.

Sherman, D. 2003, 'Critical theory', in: R.C. Salomon and D. Sherman (eds.). Contionental philosophy, Blackwell.

Sim, S. 2000., *Contemporary Continental philosophy: The new scepticism.*

Swanton, C 2001, 'A virtue ethical account of the right action', *Ethics* 112, pp: 32-52.

……… 2003, *Virtue ethics, a pluralistic view*, Oxford: Oxford University Press.

……… 2013 'The definition of virtue ethics', in: D.C. Russell, (ed.), *The Cambridge.*

Snow, N. 2020, *Contemporary virtue ethics,* Cambridge: Cambridge University Press.

……… 'Neo-Aristotelian virtue ethics' 2018, in N. Snow (ed.), *The Oxford handbook of virtue,* Oxford: Oxford University Press.

Taminiaux, J.1994, 'Philosophy of existence 1: Heidegger', in Kearny, R. (ed), *Continental` philosophyin the 20th century,* Milton Park: Routledge: p.38-73.

Taylor, C. 2003, *Rorty and philosophy,* in: Guignon, C. and D. Hiley (eds.), *Richard Rorty*, Cambridge University Press.

Tomasello, M. 2016, *A natural history of human morality*, Cambridge, MA: Harvard University Press.

Vygotski, 1962, *Thought and language,* ed and tr by E. Hanfmann and G Varkar, Cambridge: MIT Press.

Wall, J. 2003, 'Phronesis, poetics and moral credibility', *Ethical Theory and Moral practice,*

Welchman, J. (ed.) 2006, *The practice of virtue,* Indianapolis: Hackett.

……… 2006a, Introduction, in Welchman (ed.) 2006, pp. ix-xxv.

……… 2013, 'Virtue ethics and the right action', in: D.C. Russell, (ed.), *The Cambridge companion to virtue ethics,* Cambridge: Cambridge University Press, pp.172-96.

Wirth, J.M. 2005, *Schelling now: Contemporary readings,* Indiana University Press.

Williams, M. 2003, 'Rorty on knowledge and truth', in: Guignon, C. and D. Hiley (eds.), *Richard Rorty*, Cambridge University Press.

Zhuangzi, translated into Dutch and clarified by K. Schipper 2007, Amsterdam.

Van Zyl, L.2002, 'Virtue theory and applied ethics', *South African Journal of Philosophy,* 21/2 : 133-43.